HOW TO THINK
POLITICALLY

HOW TO THINK POLITICALLY

Sages, Scholars and Statesmen Whose
Ideas Have Shaped the World

GRAEME GARRARD

AND

JAMES BERNARD MURPHY

BLOOMSBURY CONTINUUM
LONDON • NEW YORK • OXFORD • NEW DELHI • SYDNEY

BLOOMSBURY CONTINUUM
Bloomsbury Publishing Plc
50 Bedford Square, London, WC1B 3DP, UK

First published in Great Britain 2019

A catalogue record for this book is available from the British Library

Library of Congress Cataloguing-in-Publication data has been applied for

ISBN: TPB: 9781472961785; EPDF: 9781472961761; EPUB: 9781472961778

2 4 6 8 10 9 7 5 3 1

Typeset by Newgen KnowledgeWorks Pvt. Ltd., Chennai, India
Printed and bound in Great Britain by CPI Group (UK) Ltd, Croydon CR0 4YY

To find out more about our authors and books visit www.bloomsbury.com
and sign up for our newsletters

To Our Students: Past, Present and Future

CONTENTS

CONTENTS

THINKER DATES

Confucius	551–479 BC
Plato	c. 428–c. 347
Aristotle	384–322
Augustine	AD 354–430
Al-Farabi	c. 872–c. 950
Maimonides	1135 or 1138–1204
Thomas Aquinas	1225–1274
Niccolò Machiavelli	1469–1527
Thomas Hobbes	1588–1679
John Locke	1632–1704
David Hume	1711–1776
Jean-Jacques Rousseau	1712–1778
Edmund Burke	1729–1797
Mary Wollstonecraft	1759–1797
Immanuel Kant	1724–1804
Thomas Paine	1737–1809
G.W. F. Hegel	1770–1831
James Madison	1751–1836
Alexis de Tocqueville	1805–1859
John Stuart Mill	1806–1873
Karl Marx	1818–1883
Friedrich Nietzsche	1844–1900
Mohandas Gandhi	1869–1948
Sayyid Qutb	1906–1966
Hannah Arendt	1906–1975
Mao Zedong	1893–1976

Friedrich Hayek	1899–1992
John Rawls	1921–2002
Martha Nussbaum	1947–
Arne Naess	1912–2009

Introduction: Politics – Might Made Right

It is fashionable today to describe politics as a swamp. For many it has become nothing more than a vulgar spectacle of deceit, ambition and opportunism. Trust in our political institutions and leaders has sunk to new lows, and politicians are held in greater contempt than for generations. Voter anger and disenchantment are growing at an alarming rate. Distracted by all the unseemly squabbling of politics, we end up allowing markets and bureaucrats to make decisions for us, leaving citizens resigned and alienated from politics-as-usual. It is very hard to imagine that ideas, let alone ideals, could play any part in all of this.

But politics has always been a messy business, governed more by expediency and compromise than by lofty ideals and principles, however much lip-service is paid to the latter. It is usually a very rough and nasty game, a 'Game of Thrones', dominated by conflicting interests, emotions, wealth and power. Much of the time it's just a low-down, dirty business, an 'evil-smelling bog', as one nineteenth-century British politician (the prime minister Lord Rosebery) called it. So shameful is political manoeuvring that it has largely been conducted behind closed doors: no decent person, it has been said, wants to observe sausages or laws being made.

This common view of politics is partially true, but it is not the whole truth. Perhaps more than in any other arena, politics shows humans at their worst *and* their best. We are all too familiar now with the worst; our book reminds readers of the best in an age when it is not often apparent, but when it needs to be, given what is at stake. In what follows we will show how politics is actually a place where ideas and ideals meet concrete reality, and where great words and great deeds mix with base motives and low intrigue.

At its best, politics can be 'a great and civilizing human activity', as the political theorist Bernard Crick described it in his defence of the art. It is the alternative to controlling people by force or fraud alone. Crick is right that politics can be and has been used for good and deliberate ends, and history provides abundant examples of this. It is capable of a moral nobility and an intellectual depth foreign to the present age of reality TV and government by Twitter, as you will see in what follows. Politics is the arena in which the fate of our planet will be decided. That is why, as citizens, we have a responsibility to engage with politics. To paraphrase Leon Trotsky: you may not care about politics but politics cares about you.

We assume that citizens should be informed. But they also need to be knowledgeable and even wise. Today we are inundated with information – but knowledge and wisdom remain as scarce as ever. Thanks to the miracles of digital technology, we are drowning in oceans of data, facts and opinions. What we need now is not more information but more insight, not more data but more perspective, not more opinions but more wisdom. After all, much of what is called information is actually misinformed, and most opinions fall short of true knowledge, let alone wisdom. Even a superficial glance at the state of contemporary politics will dispel any illusion that the explosion of information has led to wiser citizens or politicians or improved the quality of public debate. If anything, misinformation is winning out over knowledge.

How to Think Politically will help you to move beyond political information to acquire knowledge and, from there, wisdom. Information is about facts and is specific. Knowledge is more general and implies understanding and analysis. Wisdom is the highest and deepest form of insight into the reality of something. We invite you to eavesdrop upon a set of conversations among the wisest students of politics in history. In 30 short chapters you will be introduced to a diverse and fascinating cast of characters, ranging from Confucius, the wandering sage of ancient China, to Arne Naess, the modern mountaineer and ecologist, from Al-Farabi, the Muslim imam, to Hannah Arendt, the exiled German Jewish intellectual, and from Plato, the Greek philosopher, to John Rawls, the American professor.

In this book we interweave stories from the life and times of each thinker with discussion of their key insights about politics, broadly understood. All of them attempted to distil the political information of their age into genuine knowledge and to turn that knowledge into general wisdom about how to live well, as individuals and as communities. We have chosen 30 of the wisest and most influential political thinkers in history – from Asia, Africa, Europe and America. We conclude each chapter with reflections on the wisdom that each sage offers for today's political challenges.

A simple Google search will unearth an immense amount of information about the lives and ideas of these thinkers. It makes sense to start with some basic facts and opinions. But many of us crave more than that. We want to range wider and dig deeper, and to integrate all that information into a coherent and compelling understanding of politics. With over 50 years of scholarship and teaching between us, we have synthesized vast amounts of historical data and philosophical reflection into a single volume. Rather than bury you with more facts, our purpose here is to introduce you to many of the greatest political minds and ideas in history to stimulate your interest and spark your imagination.

Politics is more than merely the clash of interests. Ideas play a decisive role in human affairs, which are never purely practical. Nowhere is this more obvious than in the founding of the United States, which was as much a battle of ideas as it was a battle of arms, as were the French and Russian Revolutions. And the recent populist revolt in the West against globalization, Islam and immigration is a struggle over identity and values no less than of power and interests. That's why ideas and concepts have in some form been debated in every political system that has ever existed. The point where ideas meet reality is often a place of both cooperation and conflict, of idealism and cynicism, of hope and despair. It is there that philosophy can shed the most light on politics. Without such light, it really is just a darkling plain where ignorant armies clash by night.

No concept is more frequently associated with politics than power. What else could politics be if not the arena in which power is sought, fought over and exercised? True, power is exercised in families, churches and workplaces,

4

but supreme power is vested in governments and politics.
Government itself is sometimes defined by its monopoly
over the legitimate exercise of coercive power.

If human beings were prone to agree spontaneously
about our common life, there would be no need to exercise
power and no need for politics. But we tend to disagree,
so someone must have the power to decide when to go to
war and what taxes to impose, among other things. Power
politics is not only inevitable but also uniquely nasty and
brutal. It is a zero-sum pursuit: whatever power is gained by
one person or party or nation is lost by another. In principle,
economic activity can make everyone richer; in politics not
everyone can rule: there are always winners and losers.

If politics is the struggle over power, then how does it differ
from the behaviour of animals? After all, we see contests for
power, domination and submission throughout the animal
kingdom. Are political contests nothing more than head-
butting rituals? Are political leaders merely naked apes
asserting their dominance? Some political philosophers
do indeed compare human politics to the power struggles
of animals. According to the ancient Greek philosopher
Aristotle, however, what makes human politics unique is
that we struggle not only for power but also for justice.
Other animals can communicate pleasure or pain, but only
human language can express the differences between good
and evil, right and wrong, justice and injustice.

To see the importance of both power and justice in
politics, we can compare a government that has power
but no legitimacy to a government that has legitimacy but
no power. During the Second World War, Nazi Germany
installed many governments in the defeated nations of
Europe, possessing the power to control territory but

lacking all legitimacy or justice. At the same time, many of the legitimate governments of occupied Europe fled to London. Each of these kinds of government is fatally flawed: power without justice is often at war with its own citizens; justice without power cannot protect the rights of citizens. Who would want to live under a government that possessed only power, or under one that possessed only justice? We all expect power to be exercised justly and justice to control power.

So politics is the intersection of power and justice: power that is justified and justice that's empowered. Politics is when right is made mighty and when might is exercised rightly. The activity of politics is the attempt to bring a conception of justice to power. Of what value is a justice that is unenforced or unenforceable? Of what value is power that is not guided by justice? The first is mere fantasy and the second is mere thuggery. Justice is what gives law its 'directive force' by telling us what is right; power is what gives law its 'coercive force' by adding a sanction to ensure compliance. Were human beings perfectly good, law would need only to direct us to what is right and just; but in the face of the selfish recalcitrance of human nature, legal justice must also rely upon coercive sanctions.

The naïve idealist believes that politics is only about justice; the naïve cynic believes that politics is only about power. The great political thinkers we shall meet in this book are far from naïve in either sense; they all see politics as the intersection of justice and power, although they disagree on what justice and power are and where they should meet. Some, such as Augustine, Machiavelli, Hobbes, Nietzsche and Mao, emphasize the politics of power: Augustine compares governments to organized crime, for example, while Mao claims that political power flows from the barrel of a gun. Others, such as Plato, Aquinas, Locke, Rousseau, Paine, Kant, Mill, Rawls and Nussbaum, emphasize the politics of justice: Plato thinks that justice will arise only when philosophers rule, while Nussbaum argues that justice arises only when citizens are fully capable of self-rule.

The aspiration to justice is what makes politics noble, while the struggle for power is what makes politics sordid. Lord Acton, the great nineteenth-century historian, famously cautioned that 'power tends to corrupt and absolute power corrupts absolutely'. He was referring here to the papacy, showing that power can destroy the character of even the best of men. We are all too familiar with the moral corruption of the powerful, from the appalling depravity of Roman emperors to the bloody terror of Nazi and communist dictators. But powerlessness also tends to corrupt: schemes of justice remote from the exigencies of power tend to become utopian, irresponsible and dangerous. French and Russian political thinkers before their famous revolutions were totally powerless; as a consequence, they devised ambitious plans for the elimination of marriage, social classes, religion, property, money and the calendar. Sound political thinking depends upon a clear-sighted understanding of the demands of both justice and power. So long as citizens continue to demand that power be justified, that might be made right, we shall need political philosophers to help us understand what justice requires.

How did the great political thinkers relate to the politics of their own day? As we shall see, a few of them were pure theoreticians, remote from the exercise of power – Al-Farabi, Wollstonecraft, Kant, Hegel, Nietzsche, Arendt, Hayek and Rawls; they were either too radical or too professorial to participate directly in politics. And a few actually held political office: Machiavelli and Hume were diplomats; Burke, Tocqueville and Mill were legislators; and Madison and Mao were founders and heads of modern states. But most political philosophers were neither pure theoreticians nor actual politicians but advisers who attempted to influence the political leaders of their day. Confucius, for example, offered sage counsel to several local Chinese rulers, only to be ignored and exiled. Plato risked his life journeying to Sicily in the empty hope of shaping a local tyrant, while Aristotle gave advice to his former student Alexander the Great, who ignored it completely. Thomas Paine played a prominent role mobilizing the masses in not one but two major revolutions. In other words, most political philosophers have sought to influence the rulers of their day. But, crucially, the 30 thinkers we have chosen here did more than just that. They all wrote works that raised issues, posed questions and offered ideas about politics that transcended their immediate circumstances. As a result, they have much to say to us now. We would do well to listen to them.

History, it has been said, never repeats itself, but it does often rhyme. If we had written this book one hundred years ago, we would probably not have included several key ancient thinkers, such as Confucius, Al-Farabi and Maimonides. By the early twentieth century, history seemed to have left Confucian, Islamic and Jewish political thought behind. But, astonishingly, we have recently witnessed the revival of Confucianism in post-Mao China, the explosion of Islamic political theory across the globe and the emergence of a Jewish state in the Middle East. Today, nothing is more relevant than these once nearly forgotten thinkers. As William Faulkner reminded us: 'The past is not dead; it is not even past.' As for the future, we have chosen Arne Naess to be our final thinker, varying the chronology just a bit. His reflections upon humankind's relation to nature will only become more important over time.

Politics, as a way to manage human societies by means of argument rather than by mere force, arose relatively recently in human history and may well disappear in the future. As consumers replace citizens and as bureaucrats replace statesmen, human societies may well be governed in the future by some combination of markets and regulators. In many ways, of course, a market economy governed by technocrats would be tidier and more efficient than messy, contentious and uncertain government by politics. Consumers will be happier and government more predictable. To gauge what might be lost in such a world, you would do well to begin your journey by turning the page.

Ancients

1

Confucius: The Sage

Assassination, treachery, sedition, war and torture were normal in the feudal kingdoms of ancient China, the world's longest continuous civilization. During what is called the 'Spring and Autumn Period', which lasted from 771 to the mid-fifth century BC, hundreds of small feuding principalities were gradually consolidated by ambitious rulers into larger kingdoms. As with Renaissance Italy some two thousand years later, this time of violent political conflict was also a time of great cultural and intellectual ferment.

In the midst of the political turmoil, within and between these many warring states, Confucius sought to bring order, justice and harmony to society by offering his advice to a series of princes. Although he had some influence on a few princely rulers, especially in his home state of Lu, in general, Confucius's lifelong efforts to promote humane government led only to his own persecution and banishment, as he fled from kingdom to kingdom. Like Karl Marx in nineteenth-century Europe, he lived a life of poverty, was exiled and was barely acknowledged during his lifetime. When his favourite disciple came to visit the weary 73-year-old Confucius, seeking insight, his master could only offer a meaningful sigh of resignation.

Confucius – whom the Jesuit missionaries in China called the famous teacher 'Kongzi' ('Master Kong') – lived 25 centuries ago. Like many of the most influential teachers in world history, such as Jesus and Socrates, he never wrote anything, so our knowledge of him must be reconstructed from accounts left by his disciples and enemies, often centuries later. Hence, there will always be deep uncertainty regarding the precise nature of his teaching. Again, like Jesus and Socrates, Confucius faced persecution and failure in his own lifetime, but profoundly shaped subsequent generations, becoming by far the most influential teacher in the history of China. Later writings about Confucius, such as the *Analects*, a collection of his sayings and ideas attributed to the Great Sage by his followers, report not only what he said but also, just as importantly, what he did and how he lived.

Confucius clearly preferred an ethics of personal virtue over an ethics of rules and laws: 'Guide them by edicts, keep them in line with punishments, and the common people will stay out of trouble, but will have no sense of shame. Guide them by virtue, keep them in line with the rites, and they will, besides having a sense of shame, reform themselves.' The goal in modern Western ethics and law is to conform our deeds to a rational moral or legal standard. Although a few such maxims can be found in the reported sayings of Confucius, such as 'Do not impose upon others what you do not wish to have imposed upon yourself', Confucian thought is generally focused not upon actions but upon the character of the agent. His ethics, like that of Socrates and of Jesus, is an ethics of *being* more than it is an ethics of *doing*. Before we can do the right thing, we need to become the right person.

The challenge of a Confucian life is to become a certain kind of person: someone whose appetites, passions, thoughts and deeds are all harmonized by a fundamental attitude of goodness to all living things. But virtue involves good skills as well as a good will: the man of virtue cultivates benevolent dispositions which must be expressed in deeds of perfect propriety. This 'way' or 'path' of ethical discipline is focused on the mastery of inner passions and thoughts as well as the command of outer rituals. True benevolence requires the mastery both of self and of the social codes defining respect for every rank of person. Because Confucius's thought centres on rites, he emphasizes etiquette in all areas of life: a person's moral worth is measured by the degree of conformity to these rules, which reflect his or her own inner harmony.

Plato and Aristotle, whom we will meet very soon, developed a similar blend of aesthetic and moral ideals in their notion of 'beautiful goodness'. Virtuous conduct involves both moral goodness and nobility or beauty. It is not enough to have either good intentions or good manners. The Confucian ideal of virtue, like the ancient Greek one, is both aesthetic and moral, and relates to a person's life overall. Both ideals emphasize the essential unity of the virtues embodied in a single person of good character.

Confucius describes his own journey towards virtue in a famous passage from the *Analects*: 'At fifteen I set my heart on learning; at thirty I took my stand; at forty I came to be free from doubts; at fifty I understood the Decree of Heaven; at sixty my ear was attuned; at seventy I followed my heart's desire without overstepping the line.'

First, we see the legendary emphasis upon learning. By learning, Confucius clearly does not mean only the mastery of information. Confucian learning means 'learning by heart': that is, studying the classic stories, songs, books and poems until they are incorporated into one's deepest beliefs and desires. A Confucian scholar, says a later sage, does not annotate the classics; rather, he lets the classics annotate him. Yes, this kind of learning does involve some amount of memorization. Yet the goal is not merely to memorize but to live the classical texts. Confucianism is more than just a political theory; it is a way of life.

Second, by 'taking a stand', Confucius does not mean adopting a particular ideology but, rather, assuming the responsibilities of one's rank and station by mastering ritual propriety.

Third, 'becoming free from doubts' means much more than certainty about beliefs; it means harmonizing one's convictions with one's conduct. Becoming free from doubts means becoming free from any fear or worry; it means never suffering from psychic conflict or remorse, never being 'of two minds'.

Fourth, 'understanding the Decree of Heaven' is easy to misinterpret. Confucian ethics is not based upon obedience to the will of a personal god. Rather, Confucius seems to mean that our lives must somehow fit in with the order of the cosmos as a whole. For him, the drama of human life must accord with the larger drama of cosmic life, perhaps including fate and the sacred realm of the ancestors.

Fifth, 'my ear was attuned' draws our attention to an aesthetic or even musical dimension of virtue. The moral virtuoso is someone whose whole manner and demeanour have been shaped by the harmonies embodied in noble poetry and drama, as well as music itself. His emotions and gestures are so 'attuned' to the finest ideals of culture that his conduct can be called 'poetry in motion'.

Finally, through a lifelong effort of self-discipline and self-cultivation, the virtuous man can follow any of his desires without any fear of doing something improper. He no longer imitates any external models; he has become the model himself. His natural or spontaneous desires are fully integrated with true benevolence and ritual propriety.

There are two moral exemplars in Confucian ethics: the gentleman and the sage. Confucius normally holds up the gentleman as the proper aim of human virtue: a gentleman is a highly cultivated scholar devoted to public service. But above even the gentleman is the sage. Confucius says that he has never met a sage, though he refers to 'sage-kings' of the distant past that he admires. And he frequently denies that he himself is a sage, although later generations gave him the name 'the Great Sage'. But it is clear that a sage is the highest possible human ideal for Confucius – even though most men, he thought, should aim at becoming merely a gentleman. A gentleman is clearly an ideal of a specific culture, an idealization of a kind of enlightened nobleman; a sage is not someone defined by a particular position in the social hierarchy. In its ideal of a sage, Confucian ethics transcends the prejudices of a particular social order.

Aristotle, as we shall see, also develops the same two ethical standards: he endorses for most men the ideal of the gentleman (the 'great-souled man') but then also elevates above the gentleman the universal ideal of the philosopher or sage. Confucius, like Aristotle, partly expresses the customary ideals of his own society, but he also creates a new ideal that rises above specific times and places, providing a model for all humans. Despite his high ideals, Confucius was realistic about human nature, especially the nature of political leaders. He observed that 'I have yet to find anyone who devotes as much attention to virtue as he does to sex'.

Confucian politics, like the politics of Plato or Aristotle, is a branch of ethics. There is no separate political ethics or 'reasons of state' that would permit rulers to violate ordinary morality. In the Confucian tradition, there are five sacred relationships, each with its own set of virtues: father and son, husband and wife, older brother and younger brother, friend and friend, ruler and subject.

Each of these relationships (with the exception of friendship) is hierarchical and demands distinctive virtues of authority and obedience. The solemn duty of a ruler is to lead by his own example, which is much more important than any law or policy: 'The virtue of the ruler is like the wind; the weakness of the people is like the grass; the wind must blow over the grass.'

We don't know much about Confucius's own ideals of public affairs, but one famous passage in the *Analects* identifies three primary instruments of good government: stockpiles of weapons, stores of food and the confidence of the people. When asked about which of these goods to surrender if a ruler cannot have them all, he says 'give up arms', since food is a higher priority. But even food, he says, is less important than the confidence of the people, which is the only true foundation of good government. Confucius is reported to have endorsed low taxes on farmers so as to ensure bountiful stores of food. Despite similar violent political turmoil in ancient China and in Renaissance Italy, Confucius's focus on domestic policy and his disdain for military affairs contrasts sharply with the approach of Machiavelli, who, as we shall see, advised princes to study war above all things.

Confucianism eventually became the official ideology of Chinese rulers for almost two millennia, and Confucian texts became the basis for all education aimed at public service in China. Much more than an official ideology, the Confucian ideals of learning and of filial piety can rightly be said to form the very basis of Chinese culture. In that sense, Confucius has no parallel in the West, apart from Jesus perhaps.

Confucianism itself, however, was transformed by contact with other currents of Chinese ethical and religious thought, especially Taoism and Buddhism, into an evolving neo-Confucianism. As China began to modernize in the nineteenth century, many reformers attacked Confucianism for being feudal, patriarchal, rigid and anti-scientific. Confucian education and ritual were actively suppressed in China by the revolutionary regime of Communist leader Mao Zedong, but have enjoyed a major revival since Mao's death in 1976. Chinese culture, politics and society are still indelibly marked by millennia of Confucian thought.

What remains of Confucius's legacy? Above all, perhaps, the ideal of government led by learned men as well as the ideal of filial piety. To this day, the highest praise China's communist rulers can give to each other is: 'He never once showed disrespect to his elders.'

However, when Confucianism was officially at its lowest ebb, during the Cultural Revolution (1966–76), young Communist cadres displayed shocking disrespect and cruelty to their elders. The Cultural Revolution was Mao's attempt to mobilize China's youth to root out reactionary backsliding among their elders. But the moral chaos on display during the Cultural Revolution alerted China's communist leaders to the urgent necessity of restoring a moral ethos to Chinese society. Because China's ruling Communist Party remains officially committed to atheism, Confucianism seemed the best choice for moral education since it is not oriented towards God or the gods, and it is indigenous to China.

Today China remains ruled by 'learned guardians', but instead of the traditional literary and musical education, aspiring Chinese bureaucrats and rulers now tend to study economics and engineering. Modern China is governed by a technocratic, paternalistic elite rather than by Confucian gentlemen. What would Confucius himself say about these developments? After long silent consideration, the Master would smile wanly and sigh.

2

Plato: The Dramatist

In 399 BC the ancient Greek city-state of Athens was transfixed by the trial of Socrates. The barefoot, street-corner philosopher was notorious for asking tough questions of leading Athenian priests, generals, scholars, artists and lawyers, to see if they knew what they were talking about. Virtually no one could defend their beliefs from the demonically clever Socrates, who tied his interlocutors into verbal knots before they spluttered or blushed in humiliation. Since most people, especially eminent people, resent being made to look foolish, they responded to these Socratic 'teachable moments' in the customary human way: they conspired to kill him.

Although old, poor and grotesquely ugly, Socrates attracted as followers many young, wealthy and beautiful Athenians, who enjoyed seeing their elders skewered by the fearless philosopher. One of these young followers was Plato, who worshipped Socrates as a paragon of moral and intellectual virtue, only to look on with horror as his revered teacher, mentor and friend was condemned to death by the people of Athens.

After the death of Socrates, Plato sought to honour his beloved master by re-creating in writing the experience of Socratic conversation. Plato wrote 30 philosophical dialogues, most of which feature Socrates as a leading character. Plato was aware of the risks of attempting to represent Socratic teaching in writing, since Socrates himself never wrote anything. Indeed, Socrates claimed not even to *know* anything. He asked people questions – hoping to discover the knowledge that he himself disavowed. Socrates called himself a 'philosopher', meaning a lover of wisdom, to contrast himself with the 'sophists', who claimed to have knowledge and to teach it for a fee.

Why did Socrates teach only by conversation? Why did Plato write only dialogues? Perhaps Socrates, like his student Plato, believed that writing freezes and kills thought, rendering it like butterfly specimens in a book. In Socratic conversation and in Platonic dialogue we are treated to the living movement of thought. Socrates and Plato were sceptical about the possibility of defining truth in verbal propositions; Plato often suggests that truth is ultimately something we can only see (in our mind's eye), not say. The historical Socrates was known to be ironic and playful, half-revealing, half-concealing his own views. Plato followed the example of his teacher, so scholars today cannot agree about which views presented by Socrates represent the historical Socrates or Plato himself. In this book we will freely ascribe to Plato the views expressed in his dialogues by his teacher, Socrates.

Plato's philosophy emerges from the relationship between what Socrates says in the dialogues and what Plato shows us in the dramatic action. We see this most memorably in Plato's account of the trial of Socrates, the *Apology*. During the trial, Socrates attempts to defend himself from charges of impiety and of corrupting Athenian youth by claiming that philosophy is good both for each individual person and for the city-state as a whole. He says that 'an unexamined life is not worth living' and that Athens will never truly flourish unless it can wake up from its slumber of prejudice and ignorance. Socrates is so convinced of the importance of philosophy for his beloved Athens that, after the jury convicts him, he proposes that he be rewarded rather than punished. In response, the jury sentences him to death.

In Plato's dialogues we see both a vindication of Socrates and a warning about the hazards of mixing philosophy and politics. Plato affirms the genuine good that philosophy offers to individuals and to cities by orienting personal beliefs and public policies towards the pursuit of truth. He argues that for individuals or cities to act on unfounded beliefs is for them to stumble in the darkness of illusion and ignorance. At the same time, however, his account of the fate of Socrates reveals that philosophy can also be a danger to political communities. Politics, especially democratic politics, must rest upon shared beliefs, and it is often more important that these beliefs be shared than that they be true. Do we want citizens to take a sceptical and ironic stance towards their own democratic beliefs? Or should citizens be willing to die for beliefs that cannot withstand philosophical scrutiny? Debate plays a role in politics, but a democracy is not a debating society. Politics often depends upon decisive action made without the luxury of philosophical investigation. Plato manages to defend both the integrity of philosophy and the integrity of politics – even when they come into tragic conflict.

Are the great political philosophers able to escape the prejudices of their own time and place? The answer is a qualified yes. We saw that Confucius and Aristotle created a new ideal of the sage, whom they regarded as superior to the well-born nobles of their day. Plato, in Book Five of his dialogue the *Republic*, creates a utopian vision of a perfectly just society that could not be more sharply opposed to the Athens of his day. Plato describes three 'waves' of reform necessary for a just polity: that is, a just political community. The first wave is equal opportunity in every career for men and women. Plato proposes that women should be encouraged to become scholars, athletes, soldiers and rulers – even though women did not enjoy these opportunities in reality for another 24 centuries. He is aware that these radical ideas will be met with ridicule and abuse, which we see dramatized in the dialogue. The second wave of reform is even more startling: the rulers of the city are forbidden from owning property or even having families, so that they will promote the good of the whole city rather than their own personal wealth and children. Like soldiers, the rulers will make use only of public property, and their children will be bred and raised in common by professional nurses in public daycare centres. Finally, and most shocking of all, Plato claims that 'there will never be an end to the evils of political life unless rulers become philosophers and philosophers become rulers'. Like the other waves of reform, Plato's suggestion that philosophers should rule is met with ridicule by characters in his dialogue. Everyone, then and now, agrees that philosophers are hopeless at anything so practical as ruling. However improbable or even comical these three waves of reform may be, Plato makes it clear that only such a radical plan could protect philosophy from politics. His *Republic* is the only political regime that might not kill Socrates.

In ancient times, this dialogue was sometimes titled the *Republic or On the Just Person*, since the theme is the relationship of politics to ethics, of a just city to a just person. Plato insists that we cannot have a just city until we first have just citizens; but equally, we cannot have just citizens until we first have a just city. How do we break into this circle? Plato insists that we must expel from our ideal city everyone over ten years old, so that we can start afresh by properly cultivating the souls and bodies of young children. The only good civic education, he suggests, is to grow up in a just city. Plato argues at length that justice is primarily a harmony among the parts of the soul. Unless we create harmony within our own souls between our desires and our ideals, how can we hope to create harmony within a community? We must first become the justice we hope to create in the city.

Plato is aware of the fact that his ideal city has never existed and will never exist. But he insists that a pattern of it exists in heaven and that a truly just person will be a citizen of this heavenly city and of this city alone. We may never be able to live in a truly just political community, but we can lead our lives *as if* we did by cultivating inner harmony and treating every person we encounter justly. Plato thus offers us a vision of personal ethical goodness to guide us through the political corruption we cannot escape.

Plato developed a different way to talk about political ideals in his later dialogue, the *Statesman*. Here he notes that the rulers he described in the *Republic* govern the city by means of their wisdom, not by means of laws. Plato compares ruling a city to healing a patient: do we want our doctors to treat us according to some medical rulebook or to customize our treatments according to knowledge of our individual illnesses? He points out that the application of generic rules to individual illnesses would be a sorry form of medicine, just as the application of general laws to particular cases often leads to gross injustice. At the same time, however, if we suspected our doctors of being corrupt, then we would prefer them to be bound by the generic rules of medicine.

In the *Statesman*, Plato contrasts the ideal (best) regime, in which virtuous philosophers rule by unconstrained wisdom, with the 'second-best' regime, which assumes that rulers are not reliably virtuous and, hence, constrains them by the rule of law. Rather than aim at the best regime in theory and then settle for the second-best regime in practice, Plato says that we must aim directly at the second-best regime so as to avoid the danger of the worst regime. Paradoxically, the rule of philosophers, like the rule of tyrants, is a rule unconstrained by law. The second-best regime may not be as perfectly just as the rule of philosophers, but at least it avoids the disaster of tyranny.

A key aspect of the relation of philosophy to politics is the nature of the role that scientific expertise should play in a democracy. Across several dialogues, Plato argues that justice and good government must rest upon genuine knowledge of reality. We continue to grapple today with the challenge of bringing scientific knowledge to bear upon public policy without surrendering the ideal of popular sovereignty. To settle disputes about trade, for example, the US has a board of economists called the Federal Trade Commission. Why not have a Life and Death Commission of professional ethicists to decide disputes about abortion, euthanasia and other controversial killing? Instead of having judges and juries settle disputes, why not have engineers decide disputes about mining safety and doctors decide disputes about medical malpractice? How can we trust the judgement of judges and juries who know nothing about mining or medicine? Of course, Plato is aware that even experts can be corrupted, which is why he ultimately defended the rule of law over the rule of experts.

Today women are offered equal opportunity for success in most careers, but many women find it difficult to take full advantage of this opportunity because of the responsibilities they face raising children. Plato anticipated this dilemma when he argued that equal opportunity for women was impossible without abolishing the traditional family. According to Plato, only when women are liberated from child-rearing responsibilities will they be able to become equal with men in the workplace. If Plato had known about technologies for incubating foetuses outside of the womb, he would have embraced the idea as the final emancipation of women from child-bearing as well as child-rearing. Even when we find his proposals to be absurd or immoral, Plato always expands our imagination of the possible.

As a philosophical dramatist, Plato created a huge cast of characters who develop an astonishing range of arguments. By doing so, he set the agenda for the entire history of Western philosophy, which has been called 'a series of footnotes to Plato'.

3

Aristotle: The Biologist

Aristotle was the greatest student of Plato, who was the greatest student of Socrates. However, unlike his illustrious predecessors, Aristotle was not a native or citizen of Athens, despite living there for much of his adult life, including 20 years as a member of Plato's school, the Academy. He was born in Stagira, a town located in the Macedonian region of northern Greece. After leaving the Academy, Aristotle served as a tutor to fellow Macedonian Alexander the Great when he was an impressionable teenager. Having returned to Athens to found his own school, the Lyceum, Aristotle was later financially supported by the young Alexander. As his troops conquered the known world, Alexander sent thousands of plant and animal species back to Aristotle for research.

These associations with Macedonia came back to haunt Aristotle at the end of his life, after Alexander had died and as his empire was crumbling. In Alexander's wake a wave of anti-Macedonian sentiment swept through Athens, where the now elderly Aristotle was a conspicuous and vulnerable target. Aristotle decided to flee the city and return to his mother's home on the island of Euboea because, he said, 'I will not allow the Athenians to sin twice against philosophy', an obvious allusion to the earlier execution of Socrates. Aristotle died there peacefully very soon afterwards, another philosopher who had clashed with democratic Athens.

Aristotle was the greatest polymath in world history, the 'master of those who know', in the words of Dante. His 30 surviving treatises range in subject matter from meteorology to psychology to politics, and they dominated higher learning in the Western world until the seventeenth century. In addition to his major contributions to nearly every branch of human enquiry, Aristotle wholly invented some fields of knowledge, such as biology, formal logic and literary criticism. During the Middle Ages, as we shall see, the rediscovery of the works of Plato and Aristotle would transform Christianity, Judaism and Islam. Modern astronomy and physics arose from the efforts of Copernicus, Descartes, Galileo and Newton to refute the physical theories of Aristotle.

The portraits of Plato and Aristotle dominate Raphael's famous sixteenth-century painting *The School of Athens*. Raphael's Plato points up to the sphere of intelligible truths while Aristotle points out to the visible world. To this day, Plato is the champion of those who seek truth by pure theorizing, such as metaphysicians and mathematicians, while Aristotle inspires those who seek truth from factual research. Plato had contempt for the views of 'the many': he believed that truth would always be counter-intuitive. Aristotle, by contrast, always began his investigations with the views of ordinary people, which he then refined through interrogation. Hence, Aristotelian philosophy has long been described as 'organized common sense'.

Plato defended the most counter-intuitive of all political ideas, that philosophers should rule. Politics is characterized by the clash of opposed opinions, and Plato thought that only genuine philosophical knowledge could adjudicate and resolve clashes of opinion. Aristotle agreed that reason ought to play an important role in politics, but he distinguished the concrete practical reasoning of citizens from the abstract theoretical reasoning of philosophers. Theoretical reason aims to answer the question 'What can I know?' Practical reason, by contrast, aims to answer the question 'What shall I do?' The practical reasoning of citizens needs to be informed by the findings of theoretical reason, but practical reason relies upon experience and cannot be reduced to theoretical reason. A statesman is the exemplar of practical wisdom just as a philosopher is the exemplar of theoretical wisdom. Aristotle does not expect statesmen to be philosophers or philosophers to be statesmen.

For Aristotle, then, ethics and politics are both practical sciences, which are based upon the experience of making choices. Indeed, for him politics is a branch of ethics. In his *Nicomachean Ethics*, Aristotle says that every decision and every choice aim at some good. But, we want to object, many choices are bad. So Aristotle clarifies that every choice aims at something that appears to the agent as good. Only a mentally ill person chooses something that he or she regards as evil. Yet, of course, we often make mistakes by choosing something that appears to be good but turns out to be bad. The goods we seek vary, but they form an objective hierarchy. Some material goods are purely instrumental, such as money: we seek them only for the sake of other goods. Some goods, however, we seek for their own intrinsic enjoyment, such as knowledge or friendship. The supreme good is happiness, which everyone seeks for its own sake and never for anything else. What is happiness? According to Aristotle, it is the actualization of our potential in activities of moral and intellectual virtue. Happiness is human flourishing – not happy feelings.

But we cannot actualize our potential for moral and intellectual excellence alone. We need families, villages, schools and cities. Every community, says Aristotle in his *Politics*, arises for the sake of some good, and politics is the art of arranging social life so that every citizen can achieve moral and intellectual virtue. However, if Aristotle's ideal city-state (or *polis*) is a work of political art, it is also the product of human nature. He claims that we are by nature political animals: we realize our natural human potential only through the art of politics. As a biologist, Aristotle is certainly aware that humans are not the only social or political animals: he also mentions bees and ants. But he claims that human beings are the most political of animals because of our capacity for reasoned speech. Other animals, he says, can express pleasure or pain, but only human beings can argue about what is good or bad, just or unjust.

One way to understand a polity, says Aristotle, is to analyse its constituent elements, which are citizens. For Aristotle, a citizen is someone ready, willing and able to serve in public office, both to rule and to be ruled in turn. Hence, for him, children and the elderly are not fully citizens. Politics for Aristotle means the active participation of all citizens in deliberating, debating and deciding the issues before the community. He defines a political community as an association of rational men who share a common agreement about a good human life. His *polis* is a mutual improvement society in which citizens assist each other in achieving moral and intellectual excellence. Aristotle's ideal polity has only 10,000 citizens and has been described as a cross between a church and a university.

In addition to his famous classifications of zoological and botanical organisms into genera and species, Aristotle also collected 158 Greek constitutions and classified them. He was a biologist of politics. He first divides political regimes into those which are just and those which are unjust. Following Plato, he defines a just regime as one in which the rulers aim at the good of the whole community and an unjust regime as one in which the rulers aim at their own good alone. He cross-classifies by arguing that rulers can be one, a few or many. Hence, a just regime can be a monarchy, an aristocracy (meaning 'rule by the best') or a polity. When these regimes become corrupted, we get tyranny, oligarchy and democracy. Aristotle intends his classification to be scientific as well as ethical. He claims that his just regimes have logical priority over unjust regimes in the sense that we can only understand what is deviant or corrupt when we first understand what is healthy and just. We understand a tyrant, he says, only if we first understand a just king. Later in his treatise on *Politics*, Aristotle argues that in many cases what defines a regime is not the number of rulers but the class basis of the rulers. Hence, he defines an oligarchy as rule of, by and for the rich, while a democracy, he says, is rule of, by and for the poor. Aristotle himself seems to have preferred a regime based on the rule of the middle class, or what he called a polity. He thought the middle class more moderate and less violent than the rich or the poor.

Aristotle was a realist about politics. He assumed that virtually everyone lives in a corrupt regime. For him, the point of politics is to moderate bad government so that it does not become worse and, if possible, to try to gradually make it better. Instead of trying to turn a tyranny into a polity, he recommends reforming a tyranny into a monarchy and a democracy into a polity. In his advice to a tyrant, Aristotle describes all the nefarious tactics later associated with Machiavelli. But, unlike Machiavelli, he warns the tyrant not to resort to force and fraud, since such tyrants rarely die in bed. Instead, Aristotle advises a tyrant who wishes to reach old age to moderate his rule and act like a good king.

Aristotle's political thought is sometimes summarily dismissed by moderns on the grounds that he justified an idealized kind of natural slavery, denied that women could ever be citizens and criticized democracy. But Aristotle condemns slavery based on conquest and force: that is, the kind of slavery actually practised in ancient Athens and the US before the Civil War. Moreover, Aristotle freed his own slaves in his will. By contrast, Thomas Jefferson never freed his slaves, while the philosopher John Locke, who never owned slaves, actively promoted the slave trade. As for democracy, Aristotle forces us to ask difficult questions about our own supposed democracies. The democratic method of appointing public officials, he says, is by lottery: elections are aristocratic, since they aim to appoint the best men. And if democracy is rule by the poor, then the American regime looks more like an oligarchy, as some political scientists are now concluding. Yes, Aristotle restricted citizenship to adult freemen who actively participate in debate, decision, war and ruling. We have a more extensive conception of democracy, in which citizenship is extended to everyone born in a country; but Aristotle's democracy is more intensive, because every citizen must serve in the military and in other offices. Aristotle enables us to see what we have lost as well as what we have gained in our modern practice of democracy.

4

Augustine: The Realist

By AD 410, Rome was no longer the official capital of the empire that bore its name. Even so, when the barbarian Goths besieged and then sacked the 'eternal city', the shock was profound to the already crumbling empire whose spiritual and symbolic hub was still Rome. It was the first time in 619 years that foreign enemies had entered the city – soon after, the so-called 'Dark Ages' would descend on Europe.

The historic defeat of Rome prompted much reflection among the traumatized Romans on its causes and consequences. Although many of Rome's emperors had been Christian since the famous conversion of Constantine in 312, numerous members of the Roman elite kept to the old pagan faith, and blamed the fall of their city on the rise of Christianity. After all, Christianity champions meekness and humility; Jesus proclaimed the equality and brotherhood of all men; and many Christians had been pacifists and tax resisters. How could these new values not undermine the martial virtue and patriotism of Rome?

Was Christianity to blame for the catastrophic collapse of the Roman Empire, or were the Christians merely convenient scapegoats? To address these questions, Augustine, who was the bishop of Hippo (today Annaba, Algeria) and one of the most important and influential theologians of the early Christian Church, began work on his masterpiece, the *City of God*. As a citizen of Rome born in Roman north Africa, Augustine was also traumatized by the collapse of the empire. He began the *City of God* soon after Rome was sacked and completed the book just before another Goth army attacked and burned the walled city of Hippo.

In this book, Augustine attempts to answer the charge that Christians should be blamed for the collapse of Rome by offering a panoply of arguments. He points out, for example, that Rome's leading philosopher, Cicero, had already described the corruption of the Roman republic before the birth of Christ. Moreover, says Augustine, every Christian is a citizen of two cities, the heavenly city of God and the earthly polity in which he is born. Both cities are instituted by God, meaning that Christians have both a religious and a civic duty to uphold the institutions of the Roman empire. No doubt Christian and pagan patriotism take different forms. Augustine provides an extensive commentary on the works of the Roman historians to show that the great Roman statesmen and generals of the past were motivated by the quest for glory, the craving for domination, the love of wealth and bloodlust. In short, the virtues of the pagans were, upon examination, merely splendid vices. Christian citizens act from a nobler motive: the desire for peace and justice.

Augustine was both a Platonist and Plato's most profound critic. In Plato's *Republic*, Socrates concedes that his ideal city will never exist on earth: 'But there is a pattern of it in heaven and a just man will live by the light of the heavenly city alone.' Hence, Plato already had his own 'tale of two cities'. When Augustine reflected back upon his own youth, he recalled stealing pears from a neighbour's orchard. According to Plato's psychology, Augustine's crime must have been due to his bodily appetite overcoming his reason. Yet Augustine recalled that he and his friends never even ate the pears they stole. This insight led him to realize that Plato was wrong about the body being the source of evil. Augustine found the key to understanding his own youthful crimes in the biblical story of the fall. Eve eats the forbidden fruit not because she is hungry, but because she hopes to 'become like God'. Evil stems from the spiritual perversity of pride. True, a spiritual perversity can corrupt bodily appetite, as in the case of rape or gluttony. But to blame our bodies for evil is to blame our Creator. Augustine realized that if the body is not the source of evil, then Plato's hopes that rigorous rational and philosophical discipline could save his philosopher-kings from corruption were unfounded. Plato's rulers are as subject to the spiritual perversity of pride as anyone else.

Now we see how Augustine, a Christian idealist, could also be a political realist. Given his view that human evil is too deeply rooted to be controlled by any rational human discipline, we cannot reasonably hope for virtuous rulers. According to Augustine, politics does not stem from our good nature, as created by God: there was no politics in the Garden of Eden. Instead, politics (including war, punishment and slavery) is a necessary evil to control human sinfulness.

Augustine's grim realism about human politics is evident in his appraisal of the story of Alexander and the pirate.

Alexander the Great, as commander of a mighty fleet, encounters a lone pirate ship. He asks of the pirate: 'What do you mean by infesting the seas?' To which the pirate replies: 'What do you mean by conquering the world? You do on a large scale what I do in a tiny boat.' Augustine endorses the pirate's answer: 'What is an empire, but piracy on a large scale? What is a pirate but a small emperor?' We see Augustine's political realism in his revision of the classical definition of a political community. He cites Cicero's definition of a polity as 'an association of men united by a common understanding of right'. Unfortunately, given the fact that no pagan polity ever possessed a true understanding of justice, by Cicero's definition there never was a true polity. Augustine then goes on to propose a more realistic definition of a polity as 'a multitude of rational beings united around a common agreement on the objects of their love'. Augustine's definition of a polity here, however, might be too realistic since it includes not just pagan polities but even criminal syndicates.

Augustine's political realism has its origins in St Paul's Letter to the Romans, in which Paul says that governments are a terror not to the good but to the bad and that governments execute God's wrath upon the wrongdoer. Here the mission of government is clearly not to cultivate the moral and intellectual virtues but simply to punish malefactors. In his treatise *On Free Will*, Augustine points out that virtue rests upon the interior quality of our intentions: virtue means doing the right thing for the right reasons. But civil laws can reach only to the external deeds, not to the motives of the doer. So human laws regulate only external deeds, while the eternal law of God alone can judge the quality of our deepest intentions and motivations. Civil laws can only prohibit crimes; the eternal law prohibits all sins. Instead of attempting to create virtue and justice, the human polity should therefore aim merely at peace, since peace is the one thing that everyone seeks. As we shall see, Thomas Hobbes will follow Augustine by arguing that securing peace is the ultimate purpose of civil government. Augustine realizes that true peace is 'the tranquillity of order': the harmony within each human soul and justice between peoples. But civil peace – the mere cessation of conflict – at least permits the Church to do its work of building true peace.

In his *City of God*, Augustine argues that the love of self is the basis of the City of Man while the love of God is the basis of the City of God. He also claims that the Christian Church represents the City of God while the pagan empires represent the City of Man. But Augustine makes it clear that this identity is far from perfect: there are members of the City of God outside of the Christian Church just as there are members of the City of Man within the Christian Church. He says that he once felt the appeal of the idea of a Christian Roman empire in which the imperial City of Man could be Christianized. But he became disillusioned with the idea that there could be a Christian empire. He concluded that there was only one possible Christian society and that was the Church. Christians must learn to live in religiously pluralistic polities, so long as those polities respect the independence of the Christian Church. Augustine's ideal polity is certainly led by Christian statesmen, but he nonetheless rejected the ideal of a Christian political community.

To understand how a Christian theologian could lay the foundations for a secular conception of politics we need to recall the biblical parable of the wheat and the weeds, which was central to Augustine's political thought. A farm worker tells the farm owner that weeds are growing up amidst his wheat: 'Shall I pull up the weeds?' he asks. But the farm owner says, 'No, let the weeds and wheat grow up together; for if we try to pull up the weeds, we shall damage the wheat.' 'At the final harvest,' the owner says, 'we can separate the wheat from the weeds.'

Augustine interpreted this to mean that human beings cannot discern who belongs to the City of God and who belongs to the City of Man, since only God can discern the nature of the love within our hearts. Hence, political efforts to separate Christians from non-Christians will probably cause more harm than good. We must allow wheat and weeds to grow up together in communities of religious pluralism so that God himself can create the true City of God at the end of history. Augustine did not always respect this principle of religious tolerance himself. Notoriously, he reluctantly permitted Roman authorities to use legal and political coercion against heretics in north Africa, thus creating a dangerous precedent for the much more heinous religious persecutions of medieval and early modern Europe.

Augustine insisted that Christians would make good citizens because they feel a religious duty to obey just governments. Christians would pursue the common good without the pagan lust for personal glory. But Augustine's Christian ideals do tend to undermine some of the kinds of loyalty often thought to be central to civic virtue. For example, Augustine asks: 'Given how short is the span of human life, does it matter what kind of regime we live under, so long as we are not coerced into idolatry?' Of course, for champions of republican and democratic government, it matters a great deal. If the patriots who founded the United States had taken Augustine's point of view, America would still be a British colony.

Augustine also says of war: 'What does it matter whether those killed are our own compatriots or the enemy? It is still human blood being shed.' Yet for patriots, it matters a great deal. If we were to follow Augustine's advice, we would erect monuments not only for our own dead soldiers but also for the dead soldiers of our enemies. From the perspective of the City of God, no doubt, differences of regime are trivial and all wars are civil wars. But civic virtue in the City of Man requires more narrow loyalties.

Nonetheless, Augustine's demotion of politics from being widely honoured as the supreme human good to being regarded merely as a necessary evil continues to influence our modern attitudes to politics. When Thomas Jefferson said, 'That government governs best when it governs least', or when James Madison said, 'Were men angels, no government would be necessary', we can hear the voice of Augustine.

Medievals

5

Al-Farabi: The Imam

After supporting him for several years, Al-Farabi's patron, a famous Muslim prince of Aleppo, lost his patience. Wearing the same drab cloak everywhere, Al-Farabi was known to make cheerful observations such as 'The virtuous man is an unhappy stranger in the world and death is better for him than life'. No wonder the prince found Al-Farabi to be less than the life and soul of the party!

In retrospect, we can easily recognize Al-Farabi's poor social skills, sorry attire and asceticism as true marks of his calling as a philosopher. By eschewing any interest in financial gain or political power, Al-Farabi lived so modestly that virtually nothing is known about him, apart from his writings. These very qualities ensured his freedom and independence as a thinker. We think of an imam as a kind of Muslim cleric, but Al-Farabi boldly claimed that the only true imam is a philosopher.

Born in 870 near Farab, in modern-day Kazakhstan, Al-Farabi grew up in Damascus, lived for decades in Baghdad and died in Aleppo at the age of 80. He is revered today as the greatest of all Muslim philosophers – honoured by later Christian, Jewish and Muslim medieval philosophers as the 'Second Master' (after Aristotle). Yet Al-Farabi was also denounced by a leading medieval Islamic theologian, Al-Ghazali, as an infidel. Behind his modest demeanour was an audacious teacher. Al-Farabi attempted to introduce the ancient Greek ideal of the philosopher-king into the radically new context of an Islamic polity.

Philosophy has always been threatened by religious belief: Socrates was put to death in part because of his alleged impiety. But the challenge posed by religion to philosophy became dramatically greater in the wake of the Abrahamic religions, all of which claim to possess a divinely revealed truth independent of philosophy. If truth is contained in the Bible or the Qur'an, then what need do we have for the enquiries of philosophers?

In all of the Abrahamic faiths, we find religious fundamentalists who insist that Scripture is the only reliable source of truth. How can the fallible human enquiries of pagan philosophers possibly compare to the revealed word of God? At the same time, in all the Abrahamic religions we find rationalists who believe that philosophy alone leads us reliably to truth; they are sceptical of the truthfulness of the myths and legends of Scripture. Al-Farabi was neither a fundamentalist nor a sceptical rationalist.

Is it possible to compare claims of philosophy and religion from a neutral standpoint? Must one adopt philosophical reason to evaluate the claims of religion or adopt religious belief to evaluate the claims of philosophers? Some medieval philosophers assume the truth of Scripture and then attempt to see if the views of the philosophers can be reconciled to it; others begin with a commitment to reason and evaluate the Scripture in its light. Al-Farabi certainly looked to philosophy as the standard for judging all truth, and he devised various arguments to show that God's revelation to the Prophet Muhammad met the standards of philosophical truth.

Al-Farabi attempted to steer a middle way between religious fundamentalism and sceptical rationalism. He honoured both the revealed wisdom of the Qur'an and the rational wisdom of ancient Greek philosophy. His position could be called 'Islamic humanism', and he was attacked for it by both Islamists and humanists. How did Al-Farabi harmonize Islam and philosophy? He treated Muhammad as a philosopher, and he treated 'the divine Plato' as Scripture – that is, he argued that Muhammad understood the philosophical basis of his prophecy and that Plato's writings must be interpreted as carefully as the Qur'an. Rhetorically, of course, Plato's dialogues could not be more different from the Qur'an. But these rhetorical differences may reflect Plato's and Muhammad's different audiences more than their different views. After all, Plato did write that 'God, not man, is the measure of all things'. Perhaps Plato was Muhammad speaking ancient Greek?

Although Aristotle, as we have noted, rejected central aspects of Plato's philosophy (including his political philosophy), after Aristotle's death the 'Neoplatonists' attempted to harmonize and synthesize the ideas of Plato and Aristotle. Al-Farabi is the founder of Islamic Neoplatonism, and he devoted his life to advancing this synthesis. Although he was revered as 'the second Aristotle', his *political* philosophy is much more Platonic than Aristotelian. Indeed, Aristotle's great treatise the *Politics* was not translated into Arabic until modern times. Though Al-Farabi certainly knew of it, his own work does not draw upon Aristotle's *Politics*. Al-Farabi's political Platonism would have a fateful effect on the future of Islamic political philosophy.

Plato and Aristotle differed, as we have seen, on the question of the relationship of philosophical knowledge to politics. Aristotle contrasts the theoretical wisdom of a philosopher with the practical reason of a statesman. He insists that practical wisdom, not theoretical wisdom, is essential for good rulers. He does not expect statesmen to be philosophers or philosophers to rule.

Plato, by contrast, does not explicitly distinguish theoretical wisdom from practical wisdom. According to Plato, the evils of political life cannot cease until the masters of theoretical wisdom (that is, philosophers) rule. Of course, he also recognizes the importance of practical experience in politics, and so he insists that his philosopher-kings acquire it before ruling.

Al-Farabi decisively sides with Plato. He insists that the ideal rulers of political communities must possess both theoretical and practical wisdom. Philosopher-kings must have mastered geometry, physics, astronomy, music, metaphysics and logic. Al-Farabi believes that practical wisdom about human affairs is impossible unless it rests upon demonstrable truths about the nature of the universe and humanity's place within it. His ethics and politics revolve around a set of detailed analogies comparing the structure of the cosmos, the soul, the body and the polity. Political hierarchy, he says, must mirror the hierarchy we discover in the cosmos and in the human soul. For example, one God rules the cosmos, so one philosopher should rule the polity; reason rules the human body just as philosophy should rule society. Like Plato and Aristotle, Al-Farabi affirms natural inequality among human beings: some people are destined to rule from birth and others to be slaves.

Like Plato, Al-Farabi is aware that every actual political regime falls far short of the ideal; indeed, when have philosophers ever ruled? He carefully catalogues all the ignorant, vicious, erroneous and renegade regimes whose rulers have been dedicated not to the love of truth but to the love of wealth, honour, conquest or pleasure. Nonetheless, Al-Farabi insists that in our efforts to reform our governments we must ensure that policy rests upon philosophy: if rulers are not themselves philosophers, they can at least listen to philosophers.

Al-Farabi's great political genius was to realize that philosophers alone cannot rule. Philosophers have too little in common with ordinary people to be effective rulers. Philosophy must enlist the services of religion, law, rhetoric, literature and music in order to shape the conduct of the people in accordance with the demands of truth. Most people cannot grasp abstract ideas or follow logical demonstrations: they need visual images or verbal stories to approach the truth. Theologians, jurists, artists, writers and musicians all serve in their own way to make the truths of philosophy accessible to the people. Like Plato, Al-Farabi calls upon the poets to dress philosophical truths in pleasing garb.

By defending Plato's conception of the philosopher-king, Al-Farabi creates a real challenge to the authority of the prophet. Moses, Jesus and Muhammad are described in Scripture as divinely appointed rulers of their respective peoples. Although these prophets were all men of practical wisdom, experienced in managing human affairs, none could even remotely be described as a philosopher. If all true political authority rests upon philosophy, how does Al-Farabi account for the authority of the prophet?

The nineteenth-century German philosopher Friedrich Nietzsche disparaged Christianity as a dumbed-down 'Platonism for the masses'. Yet Al-Farabi praises Islam for bringing Platonic truths to ordinary people. His true prophet is someone who approaches the divine mind by the perfection of his rational and moral faculties. God rewards the prophet's intellectual virtue by revealing the whole of philosophical knowledge. Whereas ordinary philosophers must acquire their wisdom piecemeal through laborious enquiry and debate, prophets have their philosophical wisdom directly imparted by God. What the prophet writes in Scripture, then, is only the concrete illustration of the philosophical principles revealed by God. If Scripture is to guide human conduct, it must be accessible to ordinary people, who can understand only stories and commandments. But these stories and commandments all rest logically upon philosophical truths known to the prophets by divine revelation.

Because Scripture and the religious law it contains rest upon the implicit philosophical knowledge of the prophets, the interpretation of Scripture and its application to human affairs must be controlled by philosophers. Here we see why Al-Farabi considered the philosopher to be the true imam: all religious truth rests upon abstract principles known only to the true prophet and to his successors, the philosophers.

In addition to applying Plato's ideal of philosophical kingship to the prophetic rulers of the Abrahamic religions, Al-Farabi also applies the Platonic and Aristotelian ideal of a virtuous city-state to a large medieval empire. The ideal polity of both Plato and Aristotle is a small community of citizens united by a common vision of moral and intellectual virtue. According to the Greeks, a polity devoted to the common education of its citizens must be very small indeed – between five and ten thousand citizens. Al-Farabi was the first political philosopher to propose that this ideal could be extended to a whole nation or even an empire of nations. Indeed, he pioneered the idea of a nation as the basis of political life: does national unity rest upon a common language, ethnicity, religion, literature or music? In Islam, 'nation' refers both to a particular ethnic and cultural community as well as to 'the nation of Islam'. Al-Farabi had already witnessed the defeat of the dream of a unified Islamic empire, but he defended the idea of multi-national empires as potentially virtuous polities.

Aristotle had argued in his *Politics* that nations and empires are too large and too diverse to become communities of shared virtue. An educational polity must share a common language, religion, literature, schools and culture. Aristotle wondered how citizens could acquire the civic virtues without an opportunity to rule and be ruled in turn. According to Aristotle, size matters in politics: nations and empires are destined for vice and despotism. Yet Al-Farabi, with brilliant practical insights, considers how a ruler might create a virtuous empire while ruling a diverse set of particular nations, each with its own distinctive language, religious customs and literature.

What is Al-Farabi's legacy today? If his goal was to create an honoured place for philosophical enquiry within the schools of Islam, he was certainly successful – at least during the medieval period. If his goal was to make philosophy central to Islamic religion and politics, then he was less so. Islam, like Judaism, is fundamentally a religion of law, whose highest authorities have always been jurists. In Islam, jurisprudence, not theology or philosophy, is the queen of the sciences.

Partly because of Al-Farabi, medieval Islamic political philosophy was Platonic rather than Aristotelian. Why does this matter? Whatever his own ideals, Aristotle's *Politics* contains many arguments for democratic rule by the people. Partly because of the absence of an Aristotelian political science in Arabic, these arguments never entered the debates among medieval Islamic philosophers – indeed, arguments for popular government were very rare in the Muslim world until the nineteenth century. Perhaps this helps to explain the challenges that democratic institutions face across the Islamic world today.

The more things change, the more they remain the same. Medieval Islam was divided between religious fundamentalists and rationalist sceptics just as is today's Islam. Secular humanists during the twentieth century were convinced that religion would soon fade along with ignorance and poverty. But religion is not going to fade any time soon. Al-Farabi pioneered a middle path between religious fundamentalism and secular humanism. His Islamic humanism paved the way for the later Jewish humanism of Moses Maimonides and the Christian humanism of Thomas Aquinas. Each of these philosophers, in different ways, argued that religion must be reformed in the light of reason and that reason must be infused with the light of religion. Since the Middle Ages, we have experienced a great deal of political violence coming from religious fundamentalists as well as from secular fascists and communists. Al-Farabi, Maimonides and Aquinas all believed that religious humanism offers the best foundation for a moderate and decent politics. History has not yet proven them wrong.

6

Maimonides: The Lawgiver

As a Jewish rabbi living in Fez, Morocco, in the early 1160s, Moses Maimonides faced a horrible dilemma. The fanatical new Almohad rulers of southern Spain and the north African Maghreb demanded that all Christians and Jews either convert to Islam or die. According to one historian at the time, Maimonides feigned conversion to Islam, reciting Muslim prayers, studying the Qur'an and attending mosque. After reaching the safety of Cairo, where Judaism was tolerated, Rabbi Maimonides wrote a letter of advice to his Jewish brethren still suffering persecution in the Maghreb. Some Jews chose martyrdom rather than deny their faith, but many others converted, sincerely or not, to Islam. Maimonides compassionately argued that martyrdom, though sometimes admirable, was not required. He insisted that one could fulfil the requirements of Islamic law without repudiating one's Jewish faith. Still, he insisted that even after having 'converted' to Islam, Jews were obliged to leave their homes and journey to a land where Judaism was tolerated. God would not forsake them. No one can accuse Maimonides of hypocrisy: his words and deeds were in perfect accord.

Named after the first great Jewish lawgiver of the Bible, Moses Maimonides is widely revered today as the greatest of Jewish philosophers and jurists. But he aspired to be even more than that: he attempted to revoke and replace the whole Jewish legal tradition with his own code and, by doing so, to become the second Moses. For his presumption, Jewish traditionalists in Europe banned his writings and even burned his books.

Maimonides was born in 1138 in Cordoba, Spain – then the largest and wealthiest city in Europe as well as the centre of Islamic and Jewish learning. Two centuries of enlightened and tolerant Islamic rule had created a mecca there for scholarly and artistic exchange among Jews, Christians and Muslims. As the son of a famous scholar, Maimonides the boy quickly absorbed Jewish law and Islamic philosophy. But when he was only ten years old his Spanish utopia was destroyed by the new Almohad rulers, who suppressed Christianity and Judaism. His family spent the next 18 years fleeing from city to city within Andalusia and then from country to country across north Africa, before settling in Cairo, where his father, with whom Maimonides had originally studied the Torah, died. After leaving Cordoba, he never again enjoyed a community of intellectual peers. Even after living happily for 30 years in Cairo – where he ultimately served as court physician to the sultan, Saladin – Maimonides still referred to himself as a Spaniard.

What is surprising is not that there are very few Jewish political philosophers but that there are any. Political philosophy, after all, is a practical study of the art of ruling. Yet, for most of history, Jews have been a stateless people, ruled by foreigners. For this reason, most Jewish thought about politics has been about the internal politics of the Jewish people: how to maintain local communities within gentile polities and how to foster national identity across those polities. Jews may not have had their own political communities, but they did have their own law, courts and authorities.

Maimonides was in this sense the exemplary Jewish political leader. Soon after arriving in Cairo, he was made the head of the whole Jewish community in Egypt, responsible not only for managing Jewish life but also for maintaining close ties to other Jewish communities, especially in the Levant. True, Maimonides did not exercise full political sovereignty: he never commanded an army or a navy or ruled a state. But he levied taxes, organized relief for the poor, reformed religious liturgies and served at the head of a court of appeal to settle disputes not only within Egypt but across the Jewish Levant. Although he served only a few years in office, Maimonides acquired more political experience than most major philosophers.

Like Al-Farabi before him and Thomas Aquinas after him, Maimonides attempted to steer a middle path between religious fundamentalism and rational scepticism. He can rightly be viewed as a bridge from the Neoplatonism of the Muslim Al-Farabi to the Neo-Aristotelianism of the Christian Thomas Aquinas. It has been said of Maimonides that his heart was in Jerusalem (the original home of his faith) while his head was in Athens (the original home of philosophy). Indeed, he has been accused of using Aristotle to undermine Judaism and of using Judaism to undermine Aristotle. Scholars still cannot agree where his ultimate loyalty lay. But Maimonides himself saw no deep conflict: he insisted that Judaism was already implicitly

Aristotelian and that Aristotle was implicitly Jewish. After all, Aristotle argued that the pinnacle of human excellence is the intellectual love of God – which, says Maimonides, is also the essence of Jewish law.

Following Augustine and anticipating Aquinas, Maimonides insists that biblical faith inherently seeks rational understanding. Belief in God tends to provoke philosophical questions such as 'Who is God?' and, 'If He is so good and powerful, then why is there so much evil?' Biblical faith has always engaged in such critical self-reflection. The Hebrew prophets are already would-be philosophers, who subject biblical law and promises to scathing criticism and analysis. The whole tradition of Jewish commentary on biblical law strives to uncover the general moral principles that animate particular biblical statutes. Maimonides, then, denies that Greek philosophy is truly external to the Jewish tradition.

Faith seeks understanding, and the pinnacle of human understanding, according to Maimonides, is Aristotle. Aristotle insists that God is pure thought, with no visible properties or even emotions. According to Maimonides, so is the biblical God, who condemns all visible depictions of the divine as rank idolatry. But if the biblical God is pure thought, then why does the Bible frequently describe God in human terms, as having a 'right arm' and a 'throne' and being full of 'wrath'? According to Maimonides, most people lack the intellectual capacity to grasp invisible divine reality, so they imagine God in human terms. Like Aristotle, Maimonides insists that virtue is its own reward and vice its own punishment. But most people, he says, will not seek virtue or avoid vice unless they fear God's wrath – even though, says Maimonides, God actually has no emotions. Maimonides was not known for his humour, but he does observe: 'if we ascribe wrath to God, we run the risk of making Him angry!'

Some scholars argue that Maimonides was purely Jewish in his explication of Jewish law but purely Aristotelian in his philosophy. But it is easy to show that Maimonides was Aristotelian in his jurisprudence and Jewish in his philosophy. Aristotle argued that some laws are natural – that is, universally rational – such as 'honour your parents' or 'pay your debts'. Other laws are merely conventional and differ from polity to polity, such as what animals to sacrifice to the gods. Maimonides uses these Aristotelian ideas to analyse Mosaic laws, some of which, he says, are natural or rational (such as the prohibitions on killing and stealing), while others are purely conventional, such as those laws defining what animals to sacrifice and how many. Aristotle claims that we can understand the rational purpose of natural law but not of all conventional laws. Maimonides agrees, insisting that we can discern the rational purpose of many biblical laws, such as the prohibitions against killing and stealing, but that we shall never grasp the rationale of other biblical laws, such as the prohibitions against mixing milk and meat, or linen and wool. In short, we obey natural biblical laws because reason (as well as God) demands it, while we obey conventional biblical laws only because God demands it. Aristotle turns out to be a superb guide to Jewish law, according to Maimonides.

Just as Maimonides uses Aristotle to revise traditional Judaism, so he also uses Jewish faith to revise Aristotle. According to Aristotle, all true virtues are a mean between the extremes of excess and deficiency. For example, he insists that virtuous self-regard is a mean between the vices of arrogance (excessive self-regard) and humility (insufficient self-regard). But Maimonides insists, based on the Bible, that one cannot be too humble, since any degree of pride is a denial of God. The Bible in a sense 'teaches' Aristotle that some virtues are not means but extremes. Most controversially, Maimonides rejects Aristotle's argument that the world is eternal and insists that reason alone cannot prove whether the world is eternal or was created. In all of these ways, and in many more, he uses the light of biblical faith to revise the arguments of the philosophers, just as he uses philosophy to revise biblical faith.

Aristotle had distinguished the intellectual perfection of the philosopher from the moral perfection of the statesman. Al-Farabi then insisted that the true prophet realizes both intellectual and moral perfection, making him higher than either the philosopher or the statesman. Moreover, says Al-Farabi, the prophet combines the intellectual perfection of the philosopher with the imaginative perfection of the poet, since the prophet must be able to dress up abstract truths in vivid rhetoric, to reach all kinds of people. Maimonides develops Al-Farabi's theory of the prophet by also distinguishing intellectual from imaginative perfection. Intellectual perfection alone produces the philosopher; imaginative perfection alone produces the statesman; only the prophet combines the intellectual perfection of the philosopher with the imaginative perfection of the statesman. In other words, the prophet alone is qualified to be a philosopher-king – making the prophetic Moses a true Platonic ruler. Like Al-Farabi, Maimonides argues that a prophet is not someone arbitrarily granted miraculous powers by God but one who makes himself divine by perfecting his intellectual and moral virtue. What would be miraculous is for God to deny such a person divine revelation. Whereas Al-Farabi compares Muhammad to Moses and to Jesus as true prophets, Maimonides insists that Moses alone is the supreme prophet and lawgiver.

Centuries of commentary on the laws of Moses were compiled into books called the Talmud, which report the rabbinic debates, votes and decisions about how to apply the law to particular cases. Maimonides had the audacity (or arrogance) to attempt to systematize this vast, sprawling mass of legal material into a logically rigorous classification according to general principles. No one before or since has ever attempted comprehensively to systematize the whole of Jewish law. Maimonides's 14-volume achievement, the Mishnah Torah, can be compared only to the codification of ancient Roman law by the Emperor Justinian or the codification of modern French law by Napoleon – and those feats required the work of dozens of jurists.

Justinian's and Napoleon's codes were formally enacted and intended to revoke and replace all previous legislation, judicial decisions and commentary. Maimonides lacked the political authority to impose a new code of law upon the Jewish community. Thus, his codification presents itself as a mere digest or logical summary of Jewish law. But many Jewish jurists, then and now, suspect that Maimonides intended his new code to revoke and replace the whole of the Talmudic legal tradition – making him the new Moses, the second great Jewish lawgiver. Indeed, the title of his code, Mishnah Torah, means the Repetition of the (Mosaic) Law.

The political writer Machiavelli contrasted the founders of a political regime with its later reformers, whom he called 're-founders'. In American history, we can use this distinction to contrast the 'founding fathers' of the American regime with Abraham Lincoln, who radically reformed and 're-founded' the United States upon the principles of racial equality and strong national government. According to Machiavelli, a re-founder reforms a regime by returning it to its original principles, as Lincoln claimed he was doing by returning the United States to the principle that 'all men are created equal'.

Similarly, if Moses was the founder of ancient Israel as a political community, then Moses Maimonides aspired to be its re-founder. Just as Moses violently suppressed the idolatry of the Israelites who worshipped the golden calf, so too Maimonides violently condemned the idolatry of worshipping human images of God. The biblical Moses sought to purify the religion of the Israelites with a new code of law, just as Maimonides – the second Moses – did. Although Maimonides was not able to revoke the Talmudic tradition, his code changed for ever the way that Jewish law was to be interpreted and applied. And although Maimonides was not able to purify popular Jewish piety of its biblical imagery, he opened the door for radical philosophical critiques of biblical religion as well as radical biblical critiques of philosophy.

Today, the state of Israel finds itself deeply divided between secular humanists and religious fundamentalists, between those who seek truth only in science and philosophy and those who seek truth only in biblical law. As a revered Jewish rabbi who was also a great philosopher, Maimonides sought truth by the light of natural reason as well as by the light of revelation. Israel also finds itself in conflict with its Muslim neighbours. As a Jewish thinker who wrote his philosophical works in Arabic, Maimonides built bridges between Jews and Muslims. His work is marked by a respectful dialogue across traditions and faiths that offers hope for even the most intractable of conflicts.

7

Thomas Aquinas: The Harmonizer

When Thomas Aquinas was 19 years old, in the year 1244, he decided to take holy orders in the recently founded Dominican order of preachers. His fellow students and teachers in Naples were shocked by the sight of a young nobleman assuming the habit of an impoverished friar. Dominic founded his order to preach the Gospel and to combat heresy. For this reason, the Dominicans were at the forefront of intellectual life during the thirteenth century. Aquinas's mother opposed her son's chosen vocation and insisted that he assume his duties as the noble lord of a major estate. His brothers, who were knights in the service of the Holy Roman Emperor, kidnapped Thomas and imprisoned him in the family castle at Roccasecca for nearly two years in an attempt to force him to change his mind. They even sent young women into his cell to test his chastity. By all accounts, young Thomas's devotion to his religious vocation was unshakeable, and his family finally relented.

Aquinas, who was permitted to read philosophy and theology during his house arrest, resumed his formal studies at Paris and Cologne. Later, as an eminent theologian and philosopher, he became a confidant and adviser to King Louis IX of France and to several popes. In his philosophical masterpiece, the *Summa Theologiae*, Aquinas argued that the authority of parents over children should be limited: parents, he said, have no right to veto a grown child's decision to marry or to join a religious order.

The Middle Ages are often referred to as the 'age of authority', but they are better understood as the age of authorities, since there were several competing sources of influence. The two primary sources of intellectual authority in the thirteenth century had their origins in Athens and in Jerusalem. From ancient Greece, medieval Europe inherited the philosophy and science of Plato and Aristotle; from ancient Israel came the legacy of biblical religion, especially Christianity. Indeed, the works of Aristotle, with extensive Jewish and Islamic commentary, had just arrived in western Europe during the twelfth century. When the young Aquinas went to Cologne to study with the pioneering Aristotelian scientist and philosopher Albert the Great, he embarked upon his lifelong project of attempting to synthesize the science and philosophy of Aristotle with the claims of biblical religion. Indeed, Western civilization is best defined as a compound of Hebraism and Hellenism.

The competing claims of Athenian philosophy and the faith of Jerusalem were hotly contested in medieval Judaism, Islam and Christianity. Following in the footsteps of Al-Farabi and Maimonides, Aquinas argued that God is the author both of human reason and of revelation. Therefore, what we learn from the 'book of nature' by means of science cannot in principle contradict what we learn from the book of Scripture by means of faith. If what science teaches seems to contradict what the Bible teaches, then we must be mistaken about either the claims of science or those of the Bible. Aquinas devoted his whole intellectual life to showing that the truths found in Aristotle were consistent with the truths found in the Bible. His effort to unite Athens and Jerusalem created a third position between secular humanism and religious fundamentalism called 'Christian humanism'. Thirteenth-century scholasticism was one flowering of Christian humanism, and the Italian Renaissance was another.

Aquinas developed his view that biblical faith and Greek philosophy are compatible in the form of thousands of arguments, ranging from physics and biology to ethics, psychology and theology. His guiding principle throughout is that 'faith does not destroy or replace reason but perfects it'.

Let's briefly see how Aquinas's Christian humanism is worked out in the areas of morality and law. From Greek philosophy, he discovered the theory of moral virtues, especially what he called the 'natural virtues' of justice, wisdom, courage and moderation. Although the word 'virtue' does not appear in the Bible, these basic values are certainly mentioned, as they are in the writings of all human civilizations. Wise men and women from many different cultures have concluded that human society depends upon its members acquiring these virtues. We cannot live together in peace unless enough of us practise these virtues, and our own individual lives will go better if we act with justice, wisdom, courage and moderation.

Aquinas also discovered some virtues unique to the Bible: faith, hope and love. He called these 'supernatural virtues' because they cannot be discovered by reason alone but depend upon faith in biblical revelation. Today, secular humanists argue that we need only the natural virtues for a good human life; religious fundamentalists argue that we need only the supernatural biblical virtues. Aquinas insists that we need all of them: faith, hope and love do not replace but perfect justice, wisdom, courage and moderation. Indeed, a religious fanatic could be well described as someone who thinks that we need only faith, hope and love without justice, wisdom, courage and moderation. The supernatural virtues, without the natural, are blind; the natural virtues, without the supernatural, are austere and harsh.

In addition to the works of Aristotle, the ancient law of Rome, codified by the Emperor Justinian in the sixth century, was rediscovered in western Europe at the end of the eleventh century. The first university in Europe, at Bologna, was established precisely in order to study Roman law. (Yes, the first universities in European history were law schools.) Both secular rulers and popes set about developing codes of law inspired by the example of the Roman law. Aquinas treated Roman law as a model of rational human law, and he sought to show how it might be reconciled with the divine law revealed in the Bible. According to Aquinas, both rational human law and divine law stem from God's eternal law. Since we have no direct access to God's eternal law, we can understand it only indirectly, by means of the natural law of human conscience and the divine law of the Bible. By nature, every human being, says Aquinas, has a conscience with which he can distinguish good from bad. In addition, God reveals many basic moral truths in the Bible, both in the Old Law of Moses and in the New Law of Jesus. Why do we need biblical law if we have an innate conscience?

Aquinas tells us that our conscience is not infallible: it can make mistakes about particular judgements, and our conscience can be partly corrupted by our culture. Hence, biblical law provides a check on conscience. At the same time, our interpretations of divine law are also fallible and require the check of natural conscience. In this way, God provides human beings with two independent guides for morality: natural conscience and biblical law.

Of course, the complexity of human life requires more specific guidance than we find either in conscience or in the Bible. Our conscience tells us that wrongdoers ought to be punished, but we need human legislators to define crimes and their consequences in detail; our conscience tells us that we should drive safely, but we need precise rules of the road. A similar analysis will show that the human canon law of the Christian Church is derived from the more general principles found in the Bible. For example, the Bible tells us to 'keep holy the Sabbath', while human canon law gives us more concrete guidance by telling us to attend Mass on Sundays.

Aquinas says that the human legislator must use his practical wisdom to specify the general principles of natural law (conscience) into the particular rules of human civil law. Every human law, he says, gets its moral force by being derived from the true principles of morality in the natural law of conscience. Because valid human laws are traceable to basic moral principles, we have a duty in conscience to obey human law. An unjust law, however, is a law that violates a principle of morality – such a law loses its moral force.

In his famous *Letter from Birmingham Jail*, the Revd Martin Luther King Jr quoted Aquinas to justify his own civil disobedience: 'To put it in the terms of St. Thomas Aquinas: an unjust law is a human law that is not rooted in eternal law and natural law.' King argued that positive human laws enforcing racial subordination violate human dignity and are therefore contrary to natural law.

Dante's epic poem of the fourteenth century, *Divine Comedy*, was influenced by the works of Aquinas and can be seen as a dramatic depiction of Christian humanism. In the poem, Dante is led through the terrors of Hell and Purgatory by the ancient Roman poet Virgil, who is a symbol of natural human reason. Virgil leads Dante all the way to the gates of Heaven, but to enter, Dante must be guided by the symbol of Christian virtue, a woman named Beatrice. Natural reason is indispensable and takes us very far in our human journey, but for the final step into eternal life we need faith, hope and love. Beatrice completes what Virgil has accomplished, just as Jerusalem perfects what Athens has achieved.

Aquinas's Christian humanism could not be more relevant today, given the strident battle between secular humanists and religious fundamentalists. Many Christians, especially in the US, claim that Darwin's theory of evolution is not compatible with the account of creation in Genesis. Aquinas points out that the biblical story of God's creation of the universe in six days makes no sense if read literally, since the sun is not created until the fourth day. So a biblical 'day' cannot be what we mean by a day. Scripture does not contradict science, once properly interpreted. At the same time, many secular humanists today claim that modern science has disproved the existence of God. How is this possible, given that science can address only empirical questions, subject to observation or experiment? Clearly, science can also be misinterpreted, even by scientists. Despite many bitter skirmishes over the centuries, Aquinas would remain confident that faith and reason, religion and science, cannot come into conflict, except from human misunderstanding. God does not teach one thing in the book of nature and then contradict it in the Bible.

Moderns

8

Niccolò Machiavelli: The Patriot

Five centuries ago, at the height of the Italian Renaissance, an unemployed former civil servant sat in the study of his modest country farm in the tiny village of Sant'Andrea, just south of Florence, pouring everything he knew about the art of governing into a long pamphlet. He hoped that by making a gift of it to the city's new ruler he would win back the job he passionately loved. But it was ungraciously brushed aside by a prince who had little interest in the musings of an obscure, exiled bureaucrat on the principles of statecraft. The pamphlet was eventually published, five years after Niccolò Machiavelli's death, as *Il principe* (*The Prince*). For 14 years he had worked tirelessly and with utter devotion for his native Florence as a diplomat and public official, travelling constantly to the courts and chancelleries of Europe on its behalf where he met popes, princes and potentates. Not that this made any difference to the Medici family, who had overthrown the Florentine republic Machiavelli had so loyally served. He was promptly dismissed, arrested, tortured and exiled. The torture, six drops on the *strappado* (in which he was raised high above the ground with his arms tied behind his back on a pulley attached to the ceiling, dislocating his joints), he took admirably well, even writing some amusing sonnets about it. He only narrowly escaped execution because of a general amnesty granted when the uncle of Florence's new ruler was elected pope. Machiavelli appeared to hold few grudges. Being tortured was fair play in Renaissance politics, and he would advocate far worse in *The Prince*. But being forced out of the active life of politics that enthralled him and banished from the city he loved 'more than my own soul' was almost more than he could bear. He desperately missed the excitement, risks and constant stimulation of city life, and was bored senseless by the dreary routines of country living. He spent his days reading and writing to fend off the monotony, chasing thrushes and playing backgammon with the local innkeeper to distract himself from the stultifying dullness of provincial life.

Although only a tantalizingly short distance from the Palazzo Vecchio, the hub of Florentine government, where he had so recently worked, the exiled Machiavelli might as well have been living on the dark side of the moon. He confessed to his nephew that, although physically well, he was ill 'in every other respect' because he was separated from his beloved Florence. And he complained to a friend that he was 'rotting away' in exile. An intensely patriotic Florentine, Machiavelli spurned an offer to become an adviser to a wealthy and powerful Roman nobleman at the generous salary of 200 gold ducats, because he wanted to serve only his native city. Although he enjoyed a partial rehabilitation near the end of his life, it was in a very limited role. His glory days were over. According to popular legend, Machiavelli dreamt on his deathbed that he had chosen to remain in Hell, discussing politics with the great thinkers and rulers of antiquity, rather than suffer an eternity of tedium in Heaven with the good and the just.

Machiavelli was not a philosopher in the narrow sense of the word, or even a particularly systematic thinker. *The Prince*, which was quite hastily written in 1513, is not a rigorous philosophical treatise, which may partly explain its enduring popularity. But it has long enjoyed an exalted place in the canon of the greatest works in the history of political thought for its many penetrating insights into the nature of political life in general and the striking boldness and originality of its author's views.

The popular image of Machiavelli, one of the very few writers whose name has been turned into an adjective, is of a brutal realist who counselled rulers to cast aside ethics in the ruthless pursuit of political power. This view is not without some basis in *The Prince*, which condones murder, deceit and war as legitimate means whereby rulers can retain their grip on power and even attain glory. Machiavelli condemned tyrants who gained power but whose reigns were brutal and short, while praising those very rare statesmen above all who founded lasting states and empires, thereby achieving glory. But, for him, even power without glory is far preferable to the political norm in history: failure. History is littered with failed politicians, statesmen and rulers who either lost power because they did not appreciate the hard facts of political life or were unwilling or unable to act on them when they did.

Machiavelli tells us that, unlike Plato or Augustine, he will not offer his readers an 'imaginary republic' but will tell us the hard truth about politics as it is really practised, having seen it up close. In fact, Plato, Aristotle and Augustine saw politics up close as well, and they too understood its brutal realities. Indeed, in his *Politics*, Aristotle lists the ways that tyrants preserve power, a list that includes all of Machiavelli's recommendations. The difference is that the Ancients thought that cruelty and immorality were self-destructive while Machiavelli thought that they could be self-preserving. For Machiavelli, being insufficiently cruel is a sure path to eventual political defeat, which in Renaissance Italy was often the road to an early grave as well. He not only lived during the height of the Italian Renaissance but witnessed its unforgiving political life first-hand. It was an age of very high culture and very low politics, of Michelangelo and Cesare Borgia. What was most shocking about *The Prince* at the time was the brazen directness with which Machiavelli advocated expedients such as wiping out the entire family of a ruler, rather than the tactics themselves, which were common enough in the politics of the day.

Despite this, Machiavelli does not simply argue that politics requires that ethics be set aside, however reluctantly, in order to be effective. In the normally brutal world of real politics, rulers are often forced to choose between two evils, rather than between two goods or between a good and an evil. In such tragic circumstances, choosing the lesser evil over the greater evil, however cruel and repugnant in itself, is the ethically right thing to do. This is the classic dilemma of political ethics that is now called 'the problem of dirty hands', in which politicians are often confronted with situations in which all of the options available to them are morally reprehensible, although not all equally so. In his *Discourses on Livy*, written shortly after *The Prince*, Machiavelli states this problem and his attitude towards it very succinctly: 'if his deed accuses him, its consequences excuse him'. Indeed, for Machiavelli a hard-nosed ruler who is willing to commit evil acts (for example, deception, torture and murder) in order to prevent an even greater evil may deserve admiration and respect. Machiavelli was an ethical consequentialist, who thought that the end justified the means, rather than an amoral or immoral figure, as is commonly assumed. As opposed to setting ethics aside to gain political ends, he advocated redefining morality in terms of the ends it promotes. In politics, being fastidious about the means usually endangers the ends, which is what really matters for Machiavelli.

The truth of this was apparent to Machiavelli when he visited the town of Pistoia in Tuscany, which he recounts in *The Prince*. The town, then a Florentine colony, was torn between two rival families and on the brink of civil war. So the Florentines sent Machiavelli in to broker a settlement. When he reported back that things had gone too far and that the Florentines should step in forcefully, even bloodily if necessary, his advice was ignored for fear that it would lead to a reputation for brutality. Machiavelli's fears were soon realized when Pistoia degenerated into widespread chaos, causing much more violence and destruction than if the Florentines had taken his advice and intervened harshly earlier, which would have been the lesser evil. And, as the philosopher Kai Nielsen puts it, 'where the only choice is between evil and evil, it can never be wrong, and it will always be right, to choose the lesser evil'. It is morally right, and even obligatory, sometimes to commit acts that, while repellent in themselves, are nonetheless good in their consequences because they prevent greater evil. That is why Machiavelli calls cruelty 'well used' by rulers when it is applied judiciously in order to prevent even greater cruelty.

Such preventive cruelty is 'the compassion of princes'. Machiavellian politics is a kind of economy of violence in which successful princes commit cruel acts at the right time and in the right proportion to preserve their states and control greater evils with the judicious use of lesser ones.

One of Machiavelli's most important innovations in *The Prince* is his redefinition of the concept of virtue, which he equates with the qualities and skills necessary for political success, including ruthlessness, guile, deceit and a willingness to commit acts that would be deemed evil by conventional standards. The classical ideal of virtue that Machiavelli rejected was expressed by the ancient Roman statesman Cicero, whose *De officiis* (*On Duties*) was read and copied more frequently in the Renaissance than any other single work of classical Latin prose. Cicero argued that rulers are successful only when they are morally good, by which he meant adhering to the four cardinal virtues of wisdom, justice, restraint and courage, as well as honesty. For Cicero, the belief that self-interest or expediency conflicts with ethical goodness is not only mistaken but is deeply corrosive of public life and morals. In Renaissance Europe this idealistic view of politics was reinforced by the Christian belief in divine retribution in the afterlife for the sins and injustices committed in this life, and the cardinal virtues were supplemented by the three theological virtues of faith, hope and charity. Machiavelli believed that the ethical outlooks of both Cicero and Christianity were rigid and unrealistic, and actually caused more harm than they prevented. In the imperfect world of politics populated, as it is, by wolves, a sheepish adherence to this kind of morality would be disastrous. Men are 'ungrateful, fickle, liars and deceivers, fearful of danger and greedy for gain', in Machiavelli's words, and must be treated accordingly. Machiavellian politics is 'macho' politics, where the greatest rewards go to the boldest gamblers, namely, those who introduce new regimes rather than merely hold power for its own sake without creating anything original and enduring. Machiavelli abandons the Christian notion of divine providence in favour of the pagan conception of fate or fortune. Virtue for him is 'masculine', just as fortune is 'feminine': in *The Prince* he notoriously depicts fortune as a woman whom the man of true manliness must forcibly 'subdue' if he is to impose his will on events. While the conventional representation of fortune was feminine ('Lady Luck'), she was usually portrayed as a fairly benign trickster. In Machiavelli's hands, she becomes a fickle and malevolent goddess who delights in upsetting the plans of men and leading them into chaos and misery. Whereas Christianity preached resignation to the will of God, Machiavelli argued that a 'virtuous' ruler could impose his will on fate at least to some degree by being bloody, bold and resolute.

Machiavelli was one of the first writers in the West to state openly that 'dirty hands' are an unavoidable part of everyday politics and to accept the troubling ethical implications of this hard truth without flinching. He held that politicians who deny this are not only unrealistic but are likely to lead citizens down a path to greater evil and misery than is really necessary. It is still worth keeping this in mind today when we are tempted to condemn politicians for acts that may be wrong in a perfect world, which the world of politics is not and never will be. Sometimes doing evil is necessary to do good, as in war, and for Machiavelli politics is a kind of war. But what he thought was necessary in the cut-throat world of Italian Renaissance politics does not easily apply to modern democracies and open societies with the rule of law and a free press, by means of which governments can be constantly reviewed, scrutinized, challenged and exposed. Of course, politicians still engage in lying, corruption and wars, and there are lots of opportunities to evade detection, but the risks of doing so have grown enormously since Machiavelli's time. These changes have made parts of *The Prince* obsolete today. But that is true of all political books, to some degree, as none is *wholly* convincing. What is not true of all such books is that they retain important insights and advice that apply whatever the context, and *The Prince* is surely among the best of those exceptional works.

9

Thomas Hobbes: The Absolutist

The defining event in the long life of Thomas Hobbes was the English Civil War, which erupted in 1642, when he was in his mid-50s. Until then, he had led a quiet, low-key life of private scholarship and service to a noble family as a tutor and adviser. All of this was threatened when Oliver Cromwell and his supporters rebelled against the authority of King Charles I, plunging England into civil war. When the ever fearful Hobbes got an early whiff of trouble ahead, he became the 'first of all that fled' by removing himself to the safety of France before his homeland collapsed into open conflict. He had already spent some time there during the Thirty Years War (1618–1648), which tore Europe apart and caused unparalleled devastation, and the fearful Hobbes had no intention of hanging around in England for something similar.

Fear is the abiding theme both of Hobbes's life and of his work. Whereas Aristotle said that human beings are inclined to politics by their nature and by a passion for justice, Hobbes believed that it was fear of the state of nature that pushes us into politics. We run screaming out of the savagery of the pre-political world into the arms of any state that will protect us from its terrors. He claimed that the passions dominate reason, and that fear is the strongest of the passions. Hobbes was born in England in the year that the Spanish Armada set out to invade his country. A contemporary of his wrote that, on the morning of 5 April 1588, Hobbes's mother 'fell in labour with him upon the fright of the invasion of the Spaniards', leading Hobbes to observe that he and fear were born as twins.

After Cromwell had defeated the king (whom Hobbes initially supported) and established himself as Lord Protector of England, Hobbes quietly slipped back home from exile in France and made his peace with the new regime. But when Cromwell died and the new king (Charles II) eventually returned to England to claim his throne, Hobbes was again in a sticky position. He became a target for having abandoned the monarchy in exile, and for his alleged atheism, a dangerous position to hold in seventeenth-century England. He already had plenty of enemies who were outraged by his unorthodox political views. He was now being investigated by Parliament for heresy, but his former pupil, the new King Charles, protected his old teacher, for whom he still had affection. And so, despite having lived in very dangerous times and in fear of his life, repeatedly ending up on the wrong side of events, Hobbes survived unscathed until he was 91, an extraordinary age in the perilous seventeenth century.

Although personally timid, Hobbes displayed astonishing intellectual courage in his writings, challenging many of the reigning orthodoxies of his day. For example, he was a radical sceptic about the possibility of discovering moral or religious truths in a deeply religious and moralistic age. There is no objective moral truth to be discovered by reason since, as Hobbes observes, 'those who refer to right reason do mean their own'. Every person, he said, calls what he likes 'good' or 'just' and what he dislikes 'evil' or 'unjust'. In contrast to classical appeals to natural justice or natural reason, Hobbes looks instead to legal conventions. He compares the moral language of right, good and just to the language of arbitrary units of measurement, such as a pound or a quart. Obviously, natural reason cannot define a 'true' pound or quart, for there is no such thing. But in the realm of pure conventions what really matters is not the 'truth' of a convention but merely that there is agreement about it. Similarly, says Hobbes, what matters is that our moral, religious and political disagreements are settled, not that they are settled 'right' in an objective sense. Whoever has the power to define the meaning of a pound, a quart or what is good, just and right as they please is the sovereign. If we hope to live in some modicum of civil peace, then we must accept radical limits upon human knowledge. Reason cannot save us from violent moral, religious and political conflict; only sovereign power can. Hobbes is less concerned with who or what commands than he is that there *are* commands. Without them, we face only chaos and death.

It is often said that Hobbes's great innovation in political theory was to defend the priority of the right over the good. In the classical theories of Plato and Aristotle, the first task is to define the goods that constitute a happy and flourishing human life. Once these are identified, then justice defines our rights to those goods. Hobbes's scepticism about the goods of human life led him to reject this classical priority of the good over the right. Although no consensus is possible about human goods or virtues, he claimed, all rational people agree on the worst thing: violent death. On that fixed point of negative agreement Hobbes erects his Leviathan – the all-powerful state he named after the biblical sea monster. But he has not really reversed the priority of the good over the right. He has rejected classical conceptions of the good in favour of another conception of the good: life itself. What Hobbes gives us is really the priority of a consensus good (life) over more controversial goods, such as the moral virtues, about which we will never agree. This is the opposite of Socrates, who proclaimed that 'not life, but good life, is to be chiefly valued'.

This inalienable natural right to life is highly vulnerable without a government, because it leads to a situation where the measures I judge necessary to defend my life appear to others as threatening to them, and vice versa: what I see as defence, you see as offence. My doubts about your intentions lead me to pre-emptive strikes against you, just as your doubts motivate your aggression against me. Without a sovereign power to keep us all in 'awe', everyone becomes afraid of everyone else, an extremely volatile situation that will eventually generate violent conflict.

To make matters worse (much worse), Hobbes argues that humans are not only 'born inapt for society' but have a natural desire to control and dominate each other. We are anti-social creatures, not just a-social. We are also acquisitive beings with an insatiable lust for glory and for power that 'ceaseth only in death'. This is another reason why our natural state is conflict, a condition in which we live in constant fear of violent death. Left to our own devices in a pre-political state of nature, without an overpowering government to impose order on us and keep the peace, not only would the goods of civilization be impossible, but we would live in perpetual fear of our lives. In this state of constant and intolerable mutual fear and distrust, life is 'solitary, poor, nasty, brutish and short'. No rational person would ever remain in such a situation if they did not have to. And every rational person would pay any price, short of life itself, to escape it.

According to Hobbes, sovereign authority is established precisely to rescue us from violent controversy of the kind that plunged seventeenth-century Britain into civil war. The sovereign must have all the authority necessary, but only the authority necessary, to settle disputes from whatever source they arise. In principle, this means unlimited authority over universities, churches, families, corporations and towns as well as authority over all controversial speech and expression. But where religious, moral or political debate can be conducted without danger of erupting into violent controversy, Hobbes's sovereign has no grounds for interfering. He has a presumption for liberty, except where liberty threatens our lives, and it is the sole right and responsibility of the sovereign to decide when that is the case. The sovereign is absolute in theory but may only intervene to keep the peace, otherwise leaving us alone to pursue our own good in our own way. And a strong Hobbesian state does not need to be a large state. Indeed, it may be weakened by over-extension. The result is a rather strange combination of liberalism and authoritarianism.

Moreover, our natural right to preserve ourselves makes it legitimate sometimes to disobey the sovereign's commands. Since the only purpose for the extreme political remedy that Hobbes prescribes is to provide naturally warring individuals with an 'arbiter and judge' to keep the peace between them, it makes no sense to obey a sovereign who fails to keep you safe, either from others or from himself. For example, if the sovereign rightly orders your arrest, you are also right to attempt to evade arrest, which is why, says Hobbes, the sovereign brings armed men to arrest you. If the sovereign sentences you to death for a crime of which you are genuinely guilty, then Hobbes believes that you may legitimately try to escape, 'for no man in the institution of sovereign power can be expected to give away the right of preserving his own body'. Indeed, it would be the most rational thing to do for a guilty man sentenced to death to try to escape, since life itself is the most precious human good. Hobbes would have struggled to see Socrates's refusal to escape the death sentence that was imposed on him by his fellow citizens in Athens as the act of a rational man. Similarly, if you are commanded by the sovereign to fight against a common enemy as a conscript, then Hobbes believes that you may refuse 'without injustice', since the reason you subjected yourself to his power in the first place was to save your life, not to risk it. Here again we see a liberal core to an authoritarian political doctrine. Hobbes never expected or required his subjects to transcend their natural selfishness in political society, unlike Machiavelli, whose ideal was an intensely patriotic citizenry devoted above all to the public good. These exceptions appear to make the authority of Hobbes's sovereign less than absolutely absolute.

Hobbes prescribed an almost all-powerful sovereign, the Leviathan state, as the only way to secure peace for human beings. The basis of the highly authoritarian political system that he proposed is the consent of the governed, not God, even if the result, absolute power, is the same. Hobbes was certain that a rational person would consent to put himself under the protection of *any* ruler who could offer the peace and security of a stable political order, given the only alternative (war). Given that the state of war of all against all is the worst of all possible worlds, no price is too high to avoid it, even if that means surrendering other cherished goods and putting ourselves under an all-powerful ruler. Hobbes offered an extreme political solution to what he saw as an extreme problem. Civil war taught him to go back to political basics and spurred him to make the case for an almost all-powerful sovereign whose one, overriding purpose is to maintain peace and protect the lives of his subjects. According to Hobbes, nothing less can prevent the breakdown of civil order. Peace and security are necessary preconditions for all other goods and must therefore be secured first before other goods can be enjoyed. The first political question that any legitimate state must answer, as the modern philosopher Bernard Williams has written, is how to secure order and safety first. Everything else comes after.

There is little place in Hobbes's politics for ideals, which he considered highly dangerous, since they breed discontent with established rules and regimes and foster disagreement that can so easily escalate into conflict and even civil war. That is one reason he despised Aristotle, 'the worst teacher that ever was'. Aristotle regarded humans as naturally political beings, put virtue and happiness at the heart of political life, distinguished 'good' forms of government (as he saw them) from 'defective' forms and excluded women from participation in public life. All these influential ideas were, for Hobbes, not merely wrong but subversive of strong stable government, without which order is not possible. In Hobbes's eyes, Aristotle was really an unwitting anarchist, whose ideas about justice and virtue bred discontent with anything less than perfection, and thereby risked everything. Hobbes believed that ideas have consequences, and since most political ideas are bad, most are damaging and even dangerous. And he was one of the earliest philosophers in the history of Western thought to have treated men and women entirely as equals, and saw no reason why women should not be sovereigns.

In an age like our own, which is so vulnerable to terrorism, it is obvious that Hobbes's political views will speak very directly to many people. As the threat of terror increases (or at least the perception of a threat), it becomes more likely that people will be prepared to trade off other goods, such as freedom and privacy, for security – the first duty of the state. Hobbes understood that his arguments for unchecked political power appeal only to people who possess what he considered a rational and prudent fear of violent death. But he was aware that some people, such as those intent on dying for their cause, do not see death as the worst evil. Hobbes has no answer to the challenge posed by this, except to denounce it as irrational. Clearly, there are significant numbers of people who are not 'rational' in the Hobbesian sense. They are willing to kill and to die for their beliefs. How can such people be persuaded to accept the legitimacy of his Leviathan?

10

John Locke: The Puritan

A generation after Thomas Hobbes fled to France to escape the perils of the English Civil War, the philosopher John Locke abandoned England for the Netherlands for similar reasons. At the time, he was a scholar in Oxford with a degree in medicine. It was there that Locke became the personal physician and secretary to the Earl of Shaftesbury, who was later appointed Lord Chancellor of England. But his opposition to the reigning Stuart kings of England and Scotland placed Shaftesbury, and therefore his loyal servant Locke, under suspicion by the Crown. Eventually, Shaftesbury fled to the Protestant Netherlands, where he soon died, leaving the vulnerable Locke behind in England without the protection of his powerful patron and master. An increasingly nervous government began closing in on the Puritan Locke in the wake of a foiled plot to assassinate the king and his brother. Although not directly implicated, Locke could feel the noose tightening around his neck in pro-Stuart Oxford. When the University published a list of 'damnable doctrines' that it claimed Locke supported, he decided the time had finally come to make his escape by slipping across the Channel to the relative safety of the Netherlands.

Locke's departure only confirmed the suspicions about his loyalty back home, provoking the government there to write to the dean of his Oxford college demanding his immediate dismissal from the University. He was summoned back to Oxford to answer for himself. Locke shrewdly replied by letter instead, pleading his innocence of all the charges. His name was added to a blacklist of notable figures that King James asked the Dutch government to banish from that country for undermining the monarchy in England. Events took a dramatic turn in Locke's favour in 1688, when the Protestant king of the Netherlands led an army to Britain to overthrow the Catholic king of England, who fled in a panic. Now safe to return with William on the throne, Locke sailed back to England, where he wrote many books and essays defending liberty, religious toleration and limited constitutional government. His ideas had a huge impact on the American Founding Fathers in particular, who later had their own dispute with Britain's sovereign. The American political system they established in the late eighteenth century was, to a considerable extent, inspired by Locke's ideas about limited government, natural rights, freedom and private property. The world we live in today is therefore a Lockean world to the degree that it is an American world.

Like Hobbes before him, Locke began his reflections on the nature of government by considering what life would be like without it. His version of the hypothetical state of nature was not an intolerable war of all against all, as the pessimistic and ever fearful Hobbes had imagined it. The moderate Locke replaced Hobbes's nightmarish vision of man without government with a state of nature that was unstable and inconvenient rather than anarchic and perpetually terrifying. He thought that life without government would be far from ideal but unpleasantly tolerable. According to Locke we are naturally free and have natural ownership of our own bodies (in other words, there are no natural slaves, contrary to Aristotle's belief), but there is no common power to arbitrate the disputes and conflicts that inevitably arise in our natural condition when selfish humans interact in the absence of a state. So our freedom and our lives are vulnerable without a system of state-enforced laws to protect our natural rights. That is why Locke believed that, while such an existence is bearable, we can do better by establishing a limited government to police and protect the rights we naturally possess.

Locke's most influential political idea is that the primary reason individuals create governments is to ensure 'the preservation of their property', which is always at risk in the state of nature. By 'property', he included life itself, since we own ourselves. Originally, he reasoned, God 'gave the world in common to all mankind', so no one naturally owned anything except their own body. But God also commanded humans to labour to subdue the earth in order to improve it 'for the benefit of life'. 'Thou shalt not be idle', the Puritan Locke preached. The world exists for the use of 'the industrious and rational'. By mixing our labour with otherwise useless natural objects we turn them into useful products that can increase our wealth and wellbeing. This transforms their status from being part of the common, God-given patrimony of mankind to being the private property of the individuals who have laboured to make something of them. For Locke, we are the rightful owners of all the goods that we manufacture in this way. But our private property, no less than our lives and our freedom, is very vulnerable in the state of nature, where it is up to each of us to protect ourselves and our goods from those who do not respect them. Locke argues that government was instituted to preserve our property better by setting up a system of laws, criminal justice and force to protect our vulnerable natural rights. We would do well to surrender voluntarily our individual right to punish offenders and to execute the laws of nature to the state, which can dispense justice more impartially and effectively than each of us acting independently, in return for our obedience to its laws. This is the origin and purpose of government.

An exception that Locke makes to the sanctity of private property is in the case of someone who is forced by 'pressing Wants', such as hunger, to steal from the excess of others, as a last resort. He derives this right from the claim that 'God hath not left one Man so to the Mercy of another, that he may starve him if he please'. So, if you must steal a loaf of bread from someone who has more than they can personally consume in order to feed yourself and your family, according to Locke, then you may rightfully do so. Otherwise, theft is wrong, and it is the responsibility of the state to prevent or punish it. This exception has potentially radical implications for the global poor today, since it allows that they have a just claim to the excess of the well off if they face starvation, which millions do every year. It seems to imply the legitimacy of a radical transfer of wealth from the developed to the developing world.

Locke viewed government as a human creation established by consent and designed to serve our interests, just as Hobbes did, rather than something natural (as

Aristotle claimed) or God-given. But he favoured limited, constitutional government rather than the kind of absolutism that Hobbes insisted on. Since life without a state would not be as unbearable as Hobbes feared, Locke saw no reason to surrender ourselves completely to the sovereign, who might tyrannize us even more than we might prey on each other in the state of nature. As a result, he held that the compact establishing the state should be conditional. For Locke, the problem is less extreme than for Hobbes, and therefore so too is the solution. If the sovereign, whose purpose is to protect our life, liberty and property, does not protect these goods, then he has breached the compact that set him up in the first place, in which case we cease to have any obligation to obey him. In other words, subjects retain a right of rebellion against their rulers when they enter political society. This argument proved very attractive to the American Founding Fathers, who declared that King George III had become a tyrant, usurping their traditional rights and thereby breaching the presumed compact of government. They held that it was the king who put himself into a state of war with his American subjects, who were thereby absolved from any further obedience to him.

Like Hobbes, Locke believed that government acquires its legitimacy from the consent of the governed. This was a radical departure from what came before both of these philosophers. They held that politics is an artificial human creation established by means of a compact between people to improve their condition. However, Locke parted company from his predecessor in favouring the subordination of sovereign power to an elected legislature. For Hobbes, the sovereign alone, in the person of the king, should be the supreme power in the state who can abolish or override the democratic legislature at his discretion. A sovereign who is answerable to another power is not sovereign, by definition, and without a sovereign we are back in the unbearable state of war, according to Hobbes. Also, Locke disagreed with Hobbes that dissolving the government meant dissolving society. For Hobbes, rebelling against the state would necessarily lead to complete social breakdown as well, the worst possible outcome. But for Locke, society does not require a state to keep it together, which makes political rebellion a much less risky proposition than it was for Hobbes.

The seventeenth century was an age of constant sectarian strife and violence in Europe, as both Hobbes and Locke learned first-hand. Locke's intellectual contribution to resolving this conflict is his influential *Letter Concerning Toleration*. In it, he departs from Hobbes, who had predictably argued that the only solution to religious disagreement was for everyone in the state to conform publicly to a single, established church (in England, the Church of England). Locke instead favoured the separation of church and state, opposed as he was to the combination of force and belief. He argued that the state should tolerate religious diversity and not attempt to enforce beliefs. Care of the soul is the responsibility of religions, not of the state. This is a lesson that Locke passed on to the Founding Fathers of the United States, such as Thomas Jefferson, whose Constitution builds a legal wall between church and state. However, what Locke gave with one hand he took away with the other, by arguing that atheists should not be tolerated because promises, covenants and oaths are impossible without a belief in God. His avowed toleration also excluded Roman Catholics, whose loyalty to the state he feared would be fatally divided by their commitment to their church and its leader in Rome. Locke's was a very limited form of 'toleration', although some toleration is better than none.

Much of the everyday language of our political world today, the vocabulary of rights, property, trade and religious toleration, can be found in the seventeenth-century writings of John Locke. While the scope of legitimate state action has expanded massively since then, the liberal core that he championed remains in the form of human rights, religious freedom and constitutional government. What is missing from Locke is an appreciation of how the absolute right to unfettered accumulation of property might pose a threat to other important rights and liberties. He lived before the rise of industrial and post-industrial capitalism, and so was in no position to foresee the distortions and perverse effects that unregulated mass markets can have when they grow almost without limit. Liberalism has gradually adapted to the changing character of capitalism since Locke's day to include an expanded role for the state as a means of correcting market excesses and providing for the welfare of those who are unable to provide for themselves. But he was looking to limit state power because of the risks that it poses to individuals. Much of the debate in the democratic West today is over where the greater risk lies: the state or the market. The answer was perfectly clear to Locke in the seventeenth century, just as it was to the US Founding Fathers when they drew up a constitution in the eighteenth century to minimize the risks of tyrannical government. But what about the risks of tyrannical markets? We must look elsewhere for answers to that question.

11

David Hume: The Sceptic

David Hume's Scotland was both one of the most important centres of the eighteenth-century Enlightenment and a devoutly religious society with an established Calvinist church. Hume was a key figure of the Scottish Enlightenment, which championed religious toleration, science and trade, and was at the centre of a circle of influential philosophers and scientists that included his good friend the economist Adam Smith. He was notorious for his sceptical views on philosophy and religion, found himself caught up in the culture wars of eighteenth-century Scotland and paid a price for questioning the existence of God, miracles, the immortality of the soul and original sin. When Hume heard a man was religious, Samuel Johnson's Scottish biographer James Boswell tells us, 'he concluded he was a rascal'.

So it is hardly surprising that when Hume put himself forward as a candidate to become Professor of Philosophy at the University of Edinburgh, he was met by determined opposition from Scotland's clerical establishment, who successfully blocked him. A few years later he tried to become Professor of Philosophy at Glasgow University, a post vacated by Adam Smith. But his scholarly ambitions were again thwarted by his religious enemies, who continued to campaign against 'the Great Infidel' (as Boswell had labelled him). This culminated in the established Church of Scotland investigating Hume's 'infidel writings' in an attempt to have him excommunicated and perhaps even prosecuted for atheism, the same fate that nearly cost Hobbes his head. The proposal condemning him accused Hume of subverting religion, and thereby morality, much like the charges brought against Socrates by the Athenians. Hume was not (quite) an atheist, and never claimed to be one. He was a religious sceptic who strongly doubted the existence of God but did not believe that it is rationally possible either to affirm or deny God's existence with certainty. He was definitely anti-clerical, roundly condemning what he saw as the harmful consequences of organized religions in human history, particularly dogmatic monotheistic faiths, such as Christianity and Islam. Eventually, the proposal against Hume was dropped by the church and he was thereafter left in relative peace, although he prudently withheld publication of his attack on natural religion – the idea that the study of nature tells us something about God. Many philosophers today regard these *Dialogues Concerning Natural Religion* to be Hume's masterpiece. Their subject is still a matter of lively debate among proponents and critics of what is now called 'intelligent design'.

The book for which Hume is best known today is *A Treatise of Human Nature*, which he wrote in his twenties. To his great disappointment it 'fell dead-born from the Press', like the vast majority of scholarly books, then and now, when it initially failed to find a significant readership. He complained to a friend that it did not even 'excite a murmur among the zealots', whose hostile reaction he had hoped would at least provoke a *succès de scandale*. In fact, as we have seen, the religious zealots were excited enough by Hume's work to prevent him twice from pursuing an academic career. So he turned instead to writing a six-volume *History of England*. This became such a huge best-seller that, by the time he arrived in Paris as the Private Secretary to the British Ambassador to France, Hume, a lifelong Francophile, was a major celebrity and the toast of the salons, where he enjoyed the company of the leading French thinkers and writers of the age. They affectionately called the corpulent Scotsman 'le bon Hume' – the good Hume – for his affable nature, virtuous character and tolerant, kindly personality. The philosopher Voltaire praised Hume's *History* as 'perhaps the best ever written in any language'. The British politician Horace Walpole was less impressed and not a little jealous, confiding with annoyance to his Paris journal that 'it is incredible the homage they pay him' and adding cattily that Hume's spoken French 'is as unintelligible as his English': he spoke both languages fluently but with a strong Scottish accent that invited mockery from his admirers and detractors alike. Today, Hume's *History of England* is little read, unlike his *Treatise*, which is now regarded as one of the most important and influential works in the history of philosophy, a verdict that he did not share; he preferred to be known as a historian rather than a philosopher and even disowned the *Treatise* as a flawed work.

Hume's *Treatise* has been enormously influential in challenging the role of reason in all aspects of life and thought, contrary to the tradition of less sceptical philosophers such as Plato. Hume thought that reason remained silent on the significant ends and questions of life, incapable of telling us anything substantive about God, justice, ethics or beauty. He even concluded that 'Tis not contrary to reason to prefer the destruction of the whole world to the scratching of my finger'. He is the intellectual hero of the doubters, who have attacked the pretentions of reason and philosophy, rather than the believers, such as Hegel, who have inflated them to grand (some would say grotesque) proportions, as we shall see. The *Treatise* is the pin that sought to burst the bubble of reason. Hume portrays reason as a weak and passive faculty, the 'slave of the passions', without the power to motivate human action or guide our thinking about the ends we ought to pursue. He saw the mind as a blank slate on which sense impressions are imprinted. We have no innate knowledge of ideas, and our reason is limited to comparing our sense impressions and inferring relations between them. Hume did not regard God as a source of moral knowledge either, given the improbability of His existence and the historical unreliability of the Bible. He also denied that it is logically possible to derive moral values from natural facts, unlike Aristotle, who was an ethical naturalist. Hume famously observed in his *Treatise* how common it is for people suddenly to jump from descriptive statements (for example, 'she *is* a woman') to prescriptive statements ('therefore she *ought* not to be allowed to vote') without any bridging argument explaining how the value actually derives from the fact. Today, this common intellectual leap from 'is' to 'ought' is sometimes called the 'naturalistic fallacy' or 'Hume's Law'.

Although Hume doubted the logical validity of deriving values from facts, he offered a naturalistic psychological explanation (rather than a justification) for the existence of moral sentiments, which he claims arise spontaneously from natural human sympathy. Unlike Hobbes, Hume believed that, although we are innately selfish, we also naturally move from an idea of what someone else is feeling (for example, distress) to actually experiencing that feeling ourselves, a process he calls sympathy. Our natural sense of moral goodness and badness springs from this instinctive tendency to respond sympathetically to others (a view shared by his contemporary Jean-Jacques Rousseau, who called it 'pity'). According to Hume, we naturally approve of traits and actions that benefit not just ourselves but others as well, owing to our natural sympathy. So he was unconcerned that neither God nor reason is a source of morality, since sympathetic sentiments are part of our nature and support natural virtues of benevolence such as charity, kindness and humaneness. Natural inclination and habit mean that we unthinkingly rely on our own nature to guide us morally, without the need for God or reason. While this sounds very much like Aristotle's ethical naturalism, it is purely descriptive, not prescriptive, as Aristotle's was. Hume was accounting for the existence of apparent moral behaviour in humans, not justifying it. He does not claim that such behaviour is necessarily right, merely that it is natural. If he had concluded that it is right *because* it is natural, then he would have been guilty of the very fallacy that bears his name.

For Hume, these natural virtues have been supplemented historically by what he calls artificial virtues, such as justice, which do not arise from any natural motives. Rather, humans institute artificial virtues to solve practical problems that arise from circumstances such as the scarcity of goods and our tendency to care most about those closest to us, which can lead to social conflict. He believed that our natural feeling of benevolence towards others extends only to a limited circle of people with whom we have close relations of kinship and friendship, whereas our natural self-preference is 'insatiable, perpetual, universal, and directly destructive of society'. Therefore impartial rules of justice such as respecting private property rights and keeping promises have been devised by humans to soften and restrain our partiality. Government, 'one of the finest and most subtle inventions imaginable', is a useful corrective of our passions that makes collective life function effectively. Hume also disapproved of both severe 'monkish' Christian virtues such as celibacy, fasting and penance and the harsh spartan virtues favoured by classical republicans, such as Machiavelli and Rousseau. He preferred virtues and habits that smooth the jagged edges of our nature, soften rather than harden us and make life easier and more agreeable, an outlook entirely consistent with his own affable temperament.

Hume's philosophical radicalism led him to reject political radicalism. His generally sceptical outlook made him deeply suspicious of ambitious political schemes and projects. He had a realistic appreciation of the imperfection of societies and the limitations of human reason, which inclined him towards moderate, pragmatic reforms and gradual piecemeal change over political idealism and violent revolution, both of which he found temperamentally and philosophically uncongenial. As a sceptic, he was wary of political principles that were justified by appeals to reason or faith. He thought that rebellion was justified only in cases of 'grievous tyranny and oppression' and should not be entered into lightly. As long as institutions and rulers keep the peace and do not unduly oppress or exploit their subjects, they ought to be obeyed. Anticipating the conservative statesman and philosopher Edmund Burke, Hume cautioned any reforming leader to 'adjust his innovations as much as possible to the ancient fabric, and preserve entire the chief pillars and supports of the constitution'. Such conservatism led Thomas Jefferson to brand Hume a Tory and ban his *History of England* from the University of Virginia (which he founded). The Whig Party in Britain thought the same, viewing his *History* as Tory propaganda. On the opposite side, most Tories also regarded the work as propaganda, but against them, and the Tory Samuel Johnson dismissed Hume as an opportunist who 'has no principle'. Little wonder, therefore, that Hume complained that he was 'assailed by one cry of reproach, disapprobation and even detestation: English, Scotch, and Irish, Whig and Tory, churchman and sectary, freethinker and religionist, united in their rage' against him for one reason or another. Of his political outlook in general, Hume unhelpfully declared that 'My views of things are more conformable to Whig principles; my representations of persons to Tory prejudices'.

Hume was a proponent of the relatively genteel, urban society that flourished in his native Edinburgh during the eighteenth century. He believed that polite company, leisure, learning, trade and commerce all tend to soften and humanize people and inspire modesty and reserve, which make life more pleasant and discourage fanaticism and conflict. Rousseau, as we shall see, thought that they had the opposite effect, which is why he opposed them. Hume was in favour of freedom of the press, religious toleration and private commerce, and advocated an extended franchise (although not democracy per se), a mixed, balanced constitution and decentralized political power.

David Hume shared many of the humane values of the Enlightenment philosophers he got on with so well in Edinburgh and Paris. But he was also a philosophical radical whose doubts about the power and importance of reason subverted many of the assumptions of the Age of Reason, with which he has been closely associated. Indeed, many of the critics of that age have been inspired by Hume's deflated account of reason and his emphasis on the passions and sentiments as the ultimate motives of human action and the source of our beliefs about the ends we pursue. Such scepticism made him politically cautious, even conservative, but never reactionary. He joins a long tradition of conservative thought that warns that political theorizing in abstraction from concrete historical conditions is at best futile and at worst dangerous.

The history of our species, both before and since the eighteenth century, provides depressingly little evidence to contradict Hume's sceptical view of reason. Nor, for that matter, is there much evidence of natural human sympathy and benevolence or of the humanizing and civilizing effects of trade and commerce. On these matters, Hume's scepticism seems to have abandoned him. He appears to have had a faith in the inherent moderation and decency of human nature that is difficult to sustain against the impressive record of human folly and cruelty. But Hume's general outlook of healthy scepticism and intellectual humility may help to steer us away from some of the worst follies to which politics is too often prone.

12

Jean-Jacques Rousseau: The Citizen

When Rousseau arrived in Paris in 1742, he was a poor, unknown, unpublished, 30-year-old Genevan with little formal education (although he was well read), whose mother had died in childbirth and whose watchmaker father had abandoned him when he was just ten years old. By the time he died, 36 years later, Rousseau was a best-selling novelist, a very successful opera composer, the author of numerous books and essays on education, ethics, music, religion, language, politics, economics and even botany, the rival of Voltaire and one of the most famous men in Europe, with a cult following. It was a truly remarkable ascent. Before the end of the century, Rousseau's body lay in the Pantheon in Paris, where it had been placed by the Jacobins, the most radical of the revolutionaries, as a 'father of the French Revolution' (immediately opposite his old nemesis Voltaire, ensuring that neither would ever rest in peace). By the twentieth century, Rousseau had been blamed for influencing (if not actually causing) Romanticism, anarchism, nationalism and even totalitarianism. He remains one of the most important, influential, divisive and widely read thinkers in the history of ideas.

Rousseau once described himself as a 'man of paradoxes', which is not surprising for someone who famously claimed that it is sometimes necessary to force men to be free. He wrote a philosophical dialogue between two characters, called Rousseau and Jean-Jacques, who cannot agree about anything. His treatise on child-rearing praises maternal breast-feeding and paternal involvement with children, yet he put all five of his infant children into a foundling hospital (where most of them probably died). He claimed to have 'the greatest aversion to revolutions', yet he inspired the leaders of the French Revolution, such as Robespierre and Saint-Just, who hailed him as their hero. He is commonly included among the leading philosophers of the eighteenth-century Enlightenment, and contributed to their great project, the *Encyclopédie*, yet he praised ignorance and argued that the cultivation of the arts and sciences was detrimental to morality. Many of Rousseau's most fervent and devoted admirers in the eighteenth century were women and aristocrats, yet he was deeply sexist and professed to dislike and disapprove of wealthy 'grandees'. ('I hate their rank, their hardness, their prejudices, their pettiness, and all their vices', he thundered.) He was one of the most admired and mesmerizingly eloquent writers of his age, yet he had very little formal education and married an illiterate seamstress. He championed censorship, especially targeting the dramas of Molière, yet he admitted, 'I never miss one of his performances'. Rousseau was a popular author and musician but admired ancient Sparta, which tolerated neither writing nor music. He was the most famous writer of his age, who said 'I hate books' and claimed that they are 'good for nothing'.

Rousseau, a Calvinist Protestant by birth, like Locke, and a deist by conviction, was an enemy of Catholic Christianity, yet he modelled his autobiography on the *Confessions* of St Augustine. Like Augustine, Rousseau's influence on modern culture extends far beyond his political ideas. He created a whole new modern sensibility, a new way of thinking and feeling. Largely because of him, we value sincerity and authenticity more than any classical set of virtues. His doctrine of natural human goodness, which was interpreted as anti-Christian by his contemporaries because it denied original sin, led Rousseau to see social corruption as the root of all evil. As the founder of progressive education, he argued that children should be educated by nature, not spoiled by men. Instead of conforming to corrupting social conventions, he ate when he was hungry, slept when he was tired and dressed in unconventional clothes, which led many refined Parisians to denounce him as a barbarian. He spurned wealth, which he believed corrupted morals, and lived very simply. And he was the first person to climb the Alps just to enjoy the views, to the astonishment of his enlightened contemporaries in Paris, who saw it as further evidence of his lunacy.

Rousseau's most famous political work, *The Social Contract*, was immediately condemned by the Paris *parlement* and placed on the Vatican's Index of Forbidden Books, next to works by Maimonides, Hobbes, Locke and Hume. No one was surprised by this, least of all Rousseau. But he was shocked and dismayed when the book was banned in his native Geneva, which ordered it to be burned and its author arrested if he ever dared to set foot in the city again. This wounded Rousseau deeply, since he had always been a proud citizen of Geneva (he signed his books 'Citizen of Geneva', at least until the city authorities banned them) and claimed that he took the city's constitution as his model. He blamed the anti-clerical Voltaire, then resident near Geneva, for whipping up opposition to him in an unholy alliance with the religious bigots who dominated the city. *The Social Contract* was even proscribed in relatively liberal, tolerant Amsterdam. It seemed as though all of Europe had united against Rousseau, who was forced to flee from one country to another and even considered suicide. His desperation was so great that he actually moved to England, a nation he despised. 'I have never liked England or the English', he wrote. Even so, the English gave Rousseau sanctuary when few others would, as they later would for Marx, for which both displayed absolutely no gratitude. Rousseau even spurned the offer of a pension from King George III, which Hume had negotiated, just as he had refused a pension from King Louis XV. He had a remarkable talent for making enemies.

The Social Contract is Rousseau's most enduringly popular, widely read and influential book today, although it was not so in his own lifetime. It has been continuously in print for two and a half centuries, inspiring generations of democrats and radicals as much as it has infuriated and provoked traditionalists and conservatives such as Edmund Burke, as we shall see. It is an original blend of ancient and modern elements that is difficult to classify and has vexed its interpreters since it was published in the eighteenth century. In it Rousseau sets out the general 'principles of political right' on which regimes should be based.

Rousseau begins his political theory in the same place as Hobbes and Locke, with naturally selfish individuals in the hypothetical state of nature. In this he was fully modern. But like Machiavelli, whom he admired, he took his political models from antiquity because they understood best how to foster a powerful sense of public spirit in individuals who are naturally lacking it, something that Hobbes and Locke thought unnecessary to hold a polity together. They thought that rational self-interest alone would be a sufficient bond, whereas Rousseau believed that society would become a war of all against all unless its members could be made to identify their own interests with the public interest, as in ancient Sparta and republican Rome, regimes he admired above all others. Rousseau was a 'modern with the soul of an ancient' who half-accepted and half-rejected modernity.

In the first chapter of *The Social Contract* he famously declares that 'Man was born free, and he is everywhere in chains'. Contrary to the claims of many writers (such as Voltaire), it was never Rousseau's intention to break the bonds of political life and return us to some idyllic, pre-political state of nature. Rather, he shows how these bonds can be made legitimate so that sovereign and subject are not alienated from each other. Such alienation is the essence of despotic rule, where power is imposed by might rather than right. Rousseau gave the name 'citizen' to those who make the laws they are subject to, in what he regarded as the only legitimate form of politics. That is the only way to reconcile freedom with subjection to the law, where each individual 'obeys no one but himself, and remains as free as before'. The American Founding Fathers, such as James Madison, fundamentally mistrusted government and therefore designed a political system that was deliberately weak and limited by checks and balances. Whereas Thomas Jefferson believed that 'the government that governs least governs best', Rousseau set out to legitimize strong government rather than to limit it. Indeed, to limit a legitimate government would be to limit political right itself, which is contrary to justice. His objection to Thomas Hobbes is not, like Locke's, that he defended an absolute sovereign; it is that Hobbes defended an illegitimate sovereign. That is why Locke was more congenial to the leaders of the American Revolution than was Rousseau, the inspiration of the more radical French revolutionaries.

According to Rousseau, sovereignty should reside with the people, in the form of a 'general will', which ought to be the source of the law's legitimacy. The general will is not a mere aggregation of the wills of selfish individuals. It is only formed when citizens ask themselves what is in the common good rather than their own particular, selfish good. However, Rousseau believed that, because such public-spiritedness is wholly unnatural, it must be cultivated artificially by institutions and practices that 'turn men into citizens'. The most notorious of these is the civil religion, a religion of the state, which makes each individual 'love his duty' to the polity more than to himself, an idea he took from fellow republican Machiavelli. Both men believed that Christianity is completely unsuited to this, since it preaches 'only servitude and submission'. In fact, Rousseau says that he knows 'nothing more contrary to the social spirit' than Christianity, and nothing so 'favourable to tyranny'. Little wonder that *The Social Contract* was banned in both Calvinist Geneva and Catholic Paris.

Another device that Rousseau says is necessary to induce naturally selfish individuals to think only of the public good is what he calls 'the legislator', a concept he again shared with Machiavelli. Such rare individuals invoke God to persuade people to subordinate their particular interests to the common interest. Rousseau mentions Moses as an example: he formed the divided ancient Jews into a cohesive nation with laws he claimed were derived from God.

Despite his reputation as a naïve idealist with his head in the clouds, Rousseau was very well aware of just how unlikely it was that the political principles he set out in *The Social Contract* would ever be adopted under modern conditions. They are only applicable in relatively small, cohesive city-states of the kind commonly found in ancient Greece, and not the large, sophisticated nation-states of modern Europe, which he considered corrupt beyond redemption. In fact, he said the island of Corsica was the only place in modern Europe where his political doctrines might work. That is why it is very unlikely Rousseau would have endorsed the French revolutionary attempt to implement his theories, had he lived to see it, even though he correctly predicted that an 'age of revolutions' would soon engulf Europe.

The alienation that Rousseau experienced from the enlightened civilization in which he was immersed appears to have become complete in the last decade of his life. So he sought to escape from the company of men entirely in an apparent effort to preserve his own integrity and virtue in an age of utter corruption. He finally concluded that there is 'no hope of remedies'. He ended his days in total political resignation and pessimism, although he found some amount of personal contentment in communing with nature. His last work, the unfinished *Reveries of a Solitary Walker*, suggests that he may have come to the final conclusion that escape from civilization into rustic isolation is the only real option for the man of virtue. His identification with Socrates is best understood in terms of his own self-conception as a good man living in a wicked age, attacked and vilified because his contemporaries were blinded to his goodness by their own vice. This image is a significant part of his lasting appeal as a gadfly and social critic in the tradition of Socrates.

It is a very grave mistake to dismiss Rousseau's ideas as the ravings of a lunatic, as so many of his enemies and detractors have done over the centuries. He was undoubtedly an eccentric and often very difficult character, prone to bouts of paranoia, although he did have many powerful enemies who actively persecuted him. While his alienation from the world he inhabited was deeply personal, it was far more than simply a reaction to the times. The power and eloquence of his writing have inspired many generations of rebels, malcontents, misfits and outsiders who share his profound disquiet about the place of the individual in the modern age on so many levels.

One of Rousseau's most profound influences on modern thought was to replace the ancient vocabulary of the virtues and vices with the modern ideas of sincerity and authenticity. If we now strive to be true to ourselves, to act with integrity rather than to emulate ancient role models, then we are followers of Rousseau, for better or worse. Another of his great influences has been his very powerful and eloquent defence of the idea of popular sovereignty, that the people are the ultimate source of political legitimacy, whose will should guide the state without qualification. This populist message resonated very powerfully with ordinary people disenchanted with corrupt and self-serving elites across Europe in the eighteenth and nineteenth centuries, starting in the French Revolution. The recent return of populist politics and the growing anger at a system that favours the rich and powerful at the expense of the majority in an increasingly unequal society has made Rousseau a thinker whose time has come again.

13

Edmund Burke: The Counter-Revolutionary

By the time the French Revolution erupted in the summer of 1789, Edmund Burke was 60 years old and had been a Member of the British Parliament for a quarter of a century. He had lost his previous seat in the city of Bristol after championing a number of unpopular causes that eroded his support with the small electorate there. Burke had opposed Britain's treatment of its American colonies, had advocated a free market in corn, free trade with Ireland and Catholic emancipation (he was born, raised and educated in Ireland, the son of a Catholic mother), had campaigned for the impeachment of the corrupt governor-general of Bengal, had condemned capital punishment and had argued against unrestrained royal power and for the abolition of slavery. Obviously, Burke was no stubborn reactionary, so when the French Revolution began, his initial reaction seemed consistent with his principled advocacy of 'liberal' causes throughout his parliamentary career to that point. He first wrote that the events in Paris were a 'wonderful spectacle' whose spirit is 'impossible not to admire'. However, it wasn't long before Burke turned against the Revolution, and soon his opinion developed into a passionate rage against it which animates his famous denunciation in *Reflections on the Revolution in France*, the book for which he is still best known. At the time, most members of his own party (the Whigs) disapproved of his attack on the French Revolution, and many of his contemporaries were shocked by the vehemence of Burke's opposition, given his long career defending unpopular liberal causes. Thomas Jefferson saw Burke's *Reflections* as evidence of the 'rottenness of his mind'. But the liberals who celebrated the events in France now look rather naïve next to Burke's pessimism. At a remarkably early stage of the upheaval, when the Revolution was still controlled by moderates, he foresaw its eventual descent into terrorism, regicide, mass murder, anarchy and, finally, dictatorship.

Burke was a deeply complex and even paradoxical thinker. He was an Irishman who defended English constitutionalism, a liberal who developed the most influential attack on the French Revolution, a bourgeois who defended aristocratic privilege, a harsh critic of corrupt colonial administration in India who sat in Parliament for two different 'rotten boroughs' in the gift of his political patrons and a Protestant defender of the historic privileges of the established Church of England who sought to rally support for the beleaguered Catholic Church in France.

Although Burke's *Reflections* is focused on the French Revolution, it also transcends immediate events to present and defend a more general conception of politics and society, making it one of the most important and eloquent statements of the conservative point of view ever penned. He claims that he was 'alarmed into reflection' by the recent upheaval in France, which had prompted him reluctantly to think about the fundamental principles that should govern political life. Philosophizing about politics is not a naturally conservative impulse, since one of its key tenets, as Burke presents it, is that general abstract principles are politically dangerous. When theory and practice mix, trouble is rarely far behind, he believed, as recent events across the English Channel showed. Since the art of government is practical rather than theoretical, it is better to be governed by traditional customs and practices that evolve gradually over time than to adjust them to 'wild, visionary theories' supposedly derived from reason. Political prescriptions should be assessed for their likelihood of promoting good or evil, not for their conformity to truth or falsehood, which is an appropriate standard for philosophy but not for practical politics. 'Nothing universal can be rationally affirmed on any moral or political subject', Burke preached, but didn't quite practise and didn't really believe either.

Burke *did* affirm some universal principles of natural justice and equity. These were the basis of his harsh condemnations of British policy in Ireland, India and America. But he rejected the idea that one could reason simply and directly from the abstract rights of man to an ideal political constitution of universal applicability, as his friend and critic Thomas Paine would do. Human knowledge of the principles of justice is always tentative and fallible, which is why we must rely on our particular customs and traditions to interpret the meaning of these abstract ideals and to guide our practices. Every society will have its own interpretations of the meaning of justice, liberty and equality. For example, Burke argued that the rights of man are already incarnated in the customary and legal rights of Englishmen dating back to Magna Carta (1215), which is why he considered the grievances of the American colonists to be legitimate, as he believed that they were based on ancient customary rights that the centralizing British king did not respect. He championed gradual and piecemeal political evolution as the best way to prevent violent revolution. 'A state without the means to change', he counselled, 'is without the means of its own conservation.' By change, Burke meant small incremental steps that tweak, refine and improve the established structure of historical practices while preserving their essential core.

According to Burke, the key question that should be asked is not whether a political system conforms to some abstract ideals but whether it 'works' pragmatically, by which he meant whether it fosters peace, order and good government over the long term, given the particular context in which it is situated. The only reliable test for this is that of time, which alone can establish the true viability and durability of a political system. Burke believed that Britain had passed that test admirably well, perhaps better than any society ever had, and now needed to be protected from the revolutionary contagion that had overrun France. By contrast, the French revolutionary leaders built their politics 'not on convenience, but on truth', with predictably disastrous results. That is why the Platonic ideal of philosopher-kings is very far from Burke's view of how a polity should be governed, since politics should address immediate practical problems, not abstract problems of logic. Plato's belief that the prolonged study of mathematics is an essential prerequisite for enlightened political rule would have struck Burke as dangerously absurd. In this he was much closer to Aristotle, who distinguished very clearly between purely intellectual virtues and practical virtues, which require a flexible and pragmatic, rather than a philosophical, mind. The greatest political virtue for Burke (as for Aristotle) is prudence, which is not only the first of the political virtues but 'the director, the regulator, the standard of them all'.

Burke's *Reflections* contrasts two types of revolution, one of which he supports and the other he condemns. On the one hand, like Locke it defends the so-called 'Glorious Revolution' in 1688, in which the Catholic King James of England and Scotland was overthrown by his son-in-law the Protestant king of the Netherlands. On the other hand, he attacks the revolution in France in 1789, which overthrew the Old Regime in the name of the 'Rights of Man'. Burke was responding here to a popular sermon by the Revd Richard Price arguing that the recent revolution in France was a continuation and extension of the earlier revolution in Britain, and that both events expressed enlightened, cosmopolitan principles of freedom and progress that should be welcomed and encouraged. In Burke's eyes, the French Revolution was the very antithesis of the moderate 'Glorious Revolution' that both he and Price admired. Burke agreed with Locke that the revolution of 1688 was a welcome intervention to preserve England's ancient constitution from being usurped by the despotic tendencies of King James and his zealous royalist and Catholic supporters. Burke was convinced that the delicate balance between king, lords and commons in Britain's parliamentary form of government had evolved over centuries through a slow, piecemeal process of trial and error, compromise and pragmatism. The advantages of the traditional British approach to politics were apparent to him in the near-perfection of the British constitution, which was ideally adapted to the specific circumstances of England (if not all of Britain) and should be altered only with the greatest circumspection and humility. A wise and prudent statesman should approach long-established institutions and practices with 'a politic caution' and be guided by history and experience rather than universal doctrines about man and society. Burke strongly rejected Locke's argument that the 'Glorious Revolution' of 1688 illustrates the abstract principle that 'government exists by the consent of the governed'.

The revolution in France was something altogether different and infinitely more dangerous, as far as Burke was concerned. It was a 'philosophic revolution', abstract, utopian and universal, with a natural tendency to spread across borders like a virus, infecting the body politic wherever it went. By its very nature, 1688 was a limited, local species of revolution that did not extend beyond its territory, unlike 1789. It was, fundamentally, just a salutary correction to a basically sound political system rather than a root-and-branch change. By contrast, what happened in France was a new and radical kind of revolution – 'a Revolution of doctrine and theoretick dogma'. France after 1789 had become a 'Republic of Philosophy' governed by 'philosophic lords' full of hubris and enthralled to abstract first principles. These fanatical 'politicians of metaphysics' were intoxicated by the ideas and values of the philosophers of the Enlightenment – Voltaire, Rousseau, Condorcet, d'Alembert, Diderot, all of whom Burke denounces by name in his *Reflections*. He was among the first of the Revolution's enemies to blame the ideas of these philosophers for the disastrous collapse of political authority and social order in France in the 1790s, a view that became increasingly popular in the decades that followed. His book did much to popularize the idea of the Enlightenment as a principal cause of the Revolution.

Burke distinguished between two different conceptions of the role of elected representatives. The first is a 'delegate' who expresses his electors' will in Parliament; the second is a 'trustee' who uses his own conscience and judgement to decide what is best for the nation. In a famous speech to his own electors in Bristol, Burke promised them that, as their Member of Parliament, he would always follow his conscience as a trustee and never be a mere delegate – whereupon they promptly voted him out of office (an inconvenience that Burke easily overcame a month later, when he took the seat of Malton in Yorkshire, a 'rotten borough' in the pocket of his patron and which he likely never bothered to visit, so the question of trusteeship didn't trouble him personally again). Burke insisted that, in their deliberations, individual Members of Parliament must consider only 'one nation, with one interest, that of the whole' and not be bound by the opinions and preferences of the particular area they represent. Ironically, that was also the view of the new revolutionary regime in France, whose first written constitution expressly prohibited elected representatives from acting as delegates of their electors. The fact that only 5 per cent of the population of Britain could vote in 1790 was a mark in its favour, according to the elitist Burke, whereas for the populist Rousseau it simply proved that the country really had despotism at its heart. Students of democratic politics today continue to debate the merits of these two conceptions. When asked to choose between them, many politicians mysteriously claim to be both delegates and trustees!

The prophetic powers that Burke displayed in his *Reflections* extended far beyond the revolutionary events in France. He glimpsed a new and vulgar age emerging in Europe, dominated by 'sophisters, economists, and calculators', a trend that was just beginning in his time and is rampant in our own. His warnings about the application of ambitious, abstract theories to everyday politics without regard to context and his general political scepticism, emphasizing the delicate complexities and fragility of social life, are as relevant today as they have always been. That change should normally be undertaken with humility is an essential and eternal piece of political wisdom that Burke expressed with wonderful force and eloquence. But his horror and revulsion at the revolutionary mobs in Paris seem to have led him to a naïve trust that a traditional paternalistic elite, allied with a rising class of propertied gentlemen, would benevolently look after the wellbeing of everyone, a prominent feature of British political culture that needed little reinforcement (then or now). Such awed deference prompted Karl Marx to dismiss Burke contemptuously as a 'sycophant'. It is a criticism that Burke's contemporary Mary Wollstonecraft made a generation before Marx. His political scepticism sometimes seems suspiciously and conveniently selective.

14

Mary Wollstonecraft: The Feminist

Mary Wollstonecraft was an impoverished, 33-year-old English spinster, former governess and school headmistress when she optimistically (some would say naïvely) sailed alone to France just as the revolution she supported there was reaching its most violent and extreme phase. This was the political equivalent of storm-chasing. By then she was used to swimming against the tide of circumstances as an independent woman writer and advocate of gender equality in an age that strongly disapproved of both. Now she was voluntarily in the very eye of the revolutionary storm that was raging in Europe. She arrived in Paris just in time to see the king carried to his execution, as he 'passed by my window' on the way to the guillotine, she later recorded. The republican Wollstonecraft was surprisingly moved by this poignant image, writing to a friend that it 'made the tears flow insensibly from my eyes when I saw Louis sitting, with more dignity than I expected from his character, in a hackney coach going to meet death'. Soon it was her own head that was at risk. Barely two weeks later France declared war on Britain, and British nationals in France were rounded up in their hundreds and imprisoned as alleged spies or counter-revolutionaries. Even the radical Anglo-American writer Thomas Paine was arrested by the regime, despite being an active supporter of the French Revolution and an honorary citizen of France, appointed to the National Convention in Paris. Wollstonecraft was a friend and ally of Paine's and had every reason to expect that she too would be imprisoned and possibly even executed in the frenzy of violence that was then raging in France.

Yet, like Paine, Wollstonecraft survived the 'Reign of Terror' that followed, as the Jacobins purged France of tens of thousands of 'enemies of the state' via that efficiently 'humane' killing machine, the guillotine. 'I am grieved', she wrote ruefully to a friend, 'when I think of the blood that has stained the cause of freedom in Paris'. But her faith in the fundamental principles of the French Revolution was unbroken, and probably unbreakable. She even wrote *An Historical and Moral View of the Origin and Progress of the French Revolution* (1794) to explain and justify her optimism that a 'reign of reason and peace' would eventually rise from the horrors and excesses of the age. Unfortunately, the hope Wollstonecraft had for humanity did not extend to her own personal life. A year after writing these upbeat words she twice attempted to kill herself to relieve the pain of a broken heart. When she did eventually find contentment in her relationship with the anarchist philosopher William Godwin, it was very short-lived; she died just a few months after their marriage from complications arising from the birth of their daughter Mary, who would become the author of *Frankenstein* and the wife of the Romantic poet Percy Bysshe Shelley. Wollstonecraft was just 38.

The work for which Mary Wollstonecraft is now best known is her *Vindication of the Rights of Woman*, published the year she moved to France. It is a radical work for its time, when women in Europe had few legal rights, were excluded from public life and very tightly constrained by social norms and conventions from entering most careers and professions. For the greater part, women were confined to the domestic sphere and received little in the way of an education for anything beyond it. When a woman married, she lost most of her limited legal rights to her husband, on the traditional view that her legal personality was merged with his. That is why Wollstonecraft describes home life as often a 'gilt cage' and a 'prison' where most women cannot realize their full human potential. She suffered directly and personally from this state of affairs. That is one reason she avoided marriage until the last year of her life, despite enormous social pressure on women at the time to marry and bear children. Prior to her success as a writer, Mary Wollstonecraft was compelled to work at menial jobs that were stultifying to a woman of her natural talents and ambitions. For example, she served as the governess to a wealthy family in Ireland, a role she found demeaning and oppressive. As a single woman without means, pursuing a career as a self-supporting author in the face of such odds was a brave and risky choice, and it proved as much an inspiration to later feminists as her writings, which established her as the mother of modern feminist thought.

Wollstonecraft's best-selling *A Vindication of the Rights of Men*, which sold out in just three weeks, was her first major political work. In it she presents herself as the voice of the simple, solidly middle-class (essentially Protestant) virtues of hard work, frugality, modesty and self-discipline. She also champions Enlightenment values such as reason, progress and liberty against what she sees as Edmund

Burke's overwrought and flowery (even feminine) defence, in his *Reflections*, of tradition, aristocratic privilege and hereditary monarchy. Wollstonecraft did not offer her readers an entirely original or systematic political theory or programme in this work. She was more of a public moralist than a political philosopher in the narrow sense, closer in style to her friend and fellow radical Thomas Paine than to Thomas Hobbes. Like Jean-Jacques Rousseau, she believed that the society she inhabited was morally bankrupt and pervaded with unhappiness and hypocrisy as a result, which is why she supported the revolution in France. She thought that significant and lasting political reform was very unlikely without a fundamental moral reformation, starting with attitudes towards women.

Wollstonecraft's case for women's rights challenges the conventional separation between the public and private spheres which goes back to Aristotle and pervades virtually the whole history of Western political thought. The slogan of the twentieth-century feminist movement, that 'the personal is political', was already there in her argument that traditionally non-political institutions such as marriage and the family were the real source of the oppression of women and directly related to conventionally political issues. That is why she makes social attitudes a matter of political debate. Political rights, while necessary, are insufficient in themselves to emancipate women without a radical transformation of the wider culture and morality. For Wollstonecraft, meaningful political change is dependent on a fundamental and sweeping overthrow of traditional beliefs about the capabilities of women and on a broader moral revolution of the kind that the philosophers of the French Enlightenment that she admired had campaigned for. Although she enthusiastically supported the French Revolution, she demanded something even more radical than it was prepared to offer women, which was disappointingly little. It had failed to extend political rights to women, let alone institute a broader social revolution in gender relations. She believed that changing the relationship between citizens in the public sphere required fundamental alterations to the relationship between husbands and wives in the private sphere so that they are equal companions in a partnership, just as politics should be based on civic friendship among equal individuals of both sexes. She denounced conventional marriage as 'legal prostitution' and condemned the popular image of women as passive and frivolous adornments of their husbands, on whom they are made to depend and whose pleasure is their main purpose in life. Wollstonecraft wanted men and women to be treated the same in all spheres because treating them unequally in one would necessarily undermine equality in the others. The French Revolution was a good start, she thought, but far from sufficient to emancipate women, who were excluded from the rights of citizenship yet again.

A central theme of Wollstonecraft's *Vindication of the Rights of Woman* is the way that the education, upbringing and domestic lives of women have weakened and narrowed their minds in the process of making them pleasing to men. It has made them into 'creatures of sensation' rather than intellect, ruled by their overdeveloped passions rather than their reason, with deliberately weak and comparatively underdeveloped minds. Their unbalanced outer lives are a reflection of their unbalanced inner lives. When she writes that she hopes to persuade women 'to become more masculine', she means that she wants to enlarge and strengthen their minds so that they can think and act for themselves, just as men do. Traditional notions of femininity have stressed delicacy, sensuality and refinement, which Wollstonecraft claims have left women weak in mind and body and therefore dependent on men and unable to function outside of the domestic sphere. Her questioning of the conventional conception of gender, like her criticisms of the conventional distinction between public and private spheres, was very radical at the time and would remain so until the feminist movement in the West after the Second World War.

Wollstonecraft called for a radical transformation in the education of women as a key part of their broader political emancipation. Her first published book was *Thoughts on the Education of Daughters*, which offered its female readers practical advice on child-rearing based on solidly bourgeois values such as honesty, self-discipline and reason. Although she embraced Rousseau's progressive principles for a child-centred education, she denounced his arguments for separate, gender-based educations for boys and girls and devoted long passages in her second *Vindication* to challenging his attitude towards women in general. Despite his radical ideas about politics and education, Rousseau was in the mainstream of Western thought in his insistence on the strict separation of private and public spheres, each governed by its own principles. He believed that women posed a threat to the public sphere because they lack a natural sense of justice, and so should be kept to the private sphere. But Wollstonecraft replied that, if Rousseau is right about this lack, it is only because women have traditionally been denied access to the public sphere to develop a sense of justice and political virtue. It is a matter of bad nurture, not bad nature. She strongly opposed conventional, gender-based approaches to education in favour of a single, co-educational system, much as Plato had done in his *Republic*. Education for boys and girls should emphasize analytical thinking and practical skills that would enable everyone to lead independent lives outside the home, irrespective of sex, and which would enlarge the mind to participate actively in the duties of citizenship. Wollstonecraft insisted that the freedom and equality that should prevail in the public world must also prevail in the private realms of marriage, family and work. You cannot have one without the other, something that Rousseau and the French revolutionaries failed to understand.

The political status of women in the West, and in many places beyond it, has changed completely since the late eighteenth century. Men and women now enjoy formal civil equality and have the same legal rights and freedoms. But Wollstonecraft argued that this is not good enough. The full emancipation of women requires a revolution in the broader culture and its general attitude towards women, including established conceptions of gender. She wanted women to be given the same education and options in life as men so that they would have the same opportunity to lead fulfilling lives and develop their faculties to their fullest potential, an argument that John Stuart Mill was still making, without much success, in the late nineteenth century, as we shall see. But Wollstonecraft's belief that men and women are essentially the same is still a matter of fierce debate, not least among feminists. In the eighteenth century, she was arguing against traditionalists who believed that there are essential differences between the sexes, which were used to justify their different (and worse) treatment.

Today, the argument about essential differences is made by some feminists, who criticize Wollstonecraft for saying that women should 'become more masculine'. It is a debate involving modern science, at least to some degree, since it is as much about facts as it is about values. Given her own commitment to reason and to science, we can be sure that she would at least want us to keep our minds open to what they can tell us about the sexes.

15

Immanuel Kant: The Purist

Immanuel Kant was born in the Prussian city of Königsberg (now the Russian city of Kaliningrad), on the shores of the Baltic Sea, where he lived for all of his 79 years. It is thought that he never ventured far from his native city, which was totally destroyed in the Second World War. Here, the unmarried Kant lived a quiet, monkish life in provincial obscurity following the same undeviating daily routine decade after decade. But when he was 70 his peace was disturbed by a letter sent on behalf of the king, reprimanding Kant for his critical writings on religion. Prussia was then at war with revolutionary France, so a nervous government was cracking down on dissenting opinions. Kant, who was sympathetic to the Revolution and shared its anti-clerical views, was ordered never to publish or speak publicly about religion again. 'Failing this', the frail professor was warned, 'you must expect unpleasant measures for your continued obstinacy.' Kant obeyed, if only until the king died.

Many have been surprised by Kant's submission to the state on this occasion, which appears like a disappointing betrayal of his strong commitment to individual freedom and his devotion to the truth. As a citizen and a philosopher, he claimed, he should be free to use his reason to enlighten the public and openly to criticize established powers and laws, to 'speak truth to power', as we would say today. But as a professor at a public university, Kant was also a civil servant, and therefore felt constrained to obey the king's commands, just like a soldier who must obey orders. His advice to those torn between their rights as private individuals and their duties as public office-holders was: 'Argue as much as you want and about what you want, but obey!' Practically, this meant that minds should be free to follow reason wherever it leads, but that enacted laws and edicts of the state must finally be obeyed, even when they contradict the truth.

Recall that, 2,200 years earlier, Socrates faced a similar dilemma as both a philosopher devoted to the truth and a law-abiding citizen of Athens. Like Kant, he found himself caught between the competing demands of philosophy and politics. Socrates carried on his public philosophizing and so was eventually sentenced to death by his fellow citizens for not respecting the gods of Athens, just as Kant was threatened with 'unpleasant measures' for attacking Prussia's state religion. Yet when a friend offered to arrange for Socrates to escape from prison before his execution, the philosopher refused. He said that he had a civic duty to respect the laws under which he had long lived peacefully and freely as a citizen, even if those same laws now decreed his death. Socrates was no more of an anarchist than Kant. Argue, but obey!

Although Kant was a man of the Enlightenment, committed to freedom, open government and individual rights, he believed that revolution is never justified under any circumstances. Whatever the laws decreed by the sovereign are, they must be obeyed, since rebellion is destructive of all legal order and, as Hobbes had argued, even a bad state and bad laws are better than no state and no laws. Governments can, and should, be criticized, but they must never be overthrown. For Kant, rebelling against a tyrant is wrong 'in the highest degree', in direct contrast to Locke, who had argued that subjects are released from their obligation to obey when their rulers breach the original compact that established political society. Kant called that high treason, which should be punished by death. And only those views ought to be tolerated that do not advocate the overthrow of the constitution. He was perfectly unambiguous on this point: 'It is the people's duty to endure even the most intolerable abuse of supreme authority'.

However, for Kant, no sovereign is above the moral law, which forbids a ruler from ordering or compelling citizens to commit immoral acts such as lying and murder. Rulers should be judged by universal principles of right and publicly criticized, but still obeyed. And no sovereign should ever be punished for issuing unjust laws or for committing wrongful political actions, according to Kant, even if they can and should be judged morally. While it is not the role of the state to enforce morality, which is a personal matter, Kant wrote that it must act in a manner consistent with it. 'True politics', he said, 'cannot take a single step without first paying homage to morals'.

So what is the moral law to which everyone (including rulers) is subject, and how do we know it? For Kant it is contained in common human reason and is therefore potentially accessible to every rational person. As such, it is universal, at least for humans, since animals are not rational beings and therefore morality does not directly apply to them. Our rational nature gives us a unique status which we are required to respect in each other and in ourselves by treating humans as ends in themselves, never as means to other ends. Kant credited Rousseau with showing him that all human beings have inherent dignity. On this, he said, 'Rousseau set me right'. This is something we discover not through practical experience but by our own reason, according to Kant, making it immediately knowable and irrefutable. Morality imposes an absolute duty on everyone never to use people (including oneself) to promote other ends, since doing so reduces humans to the status of instruments rather than respecting their special character as rational beings. Governments have a duty to issue laws consistent with this moral imperative, even though, as citizens, we are never justified in rebelling against rulers who violate it.

Kant was a moral absolutist. Since morality is commanded to us by our reason, it is unconditional, meaning it must be obeyed by everyone in all situations and circumstances. It admits of no exceptions ever, any more than logic and mathematics do, since all are 'facts of reason'. Context is irrelevant. Morality consists of absolutely binding laws that are pure and categorical. That is why Kant insisted that right 'ought never to be adapted to politics, but politics ought always to be adapted to right'. There is simply no space in the Kantian moral universe, which encompasses politics, for expediency, fudge or compromise on principles, although there is an important place for prudence and flexibility *within* the boundaries of morality. For example, he believed that lying is morally wrong. This means that it is impermissible under *any* circumstances, irrespective of its consequences, which have no bearing on morality. All that matters for Kant morally is a good will, which is an internal matter for each of us, and not good consequences, which are an external matter over which we do not have control and for which we therefore have no responsibility. Whereas lying is prescribed by Machiavelli as an indispensable part of the everyday toolkit of princes, for Kant it is absolutely forbidden, even if telling the truth results in mass death and the destruction of oneself and one's state. Indeed, he occasionally went even further, commending the phrase *fiat iustitia pereat mundus* as a 'sound principle of right': let justice be done though the world be destroyed. Nothing could be further from Machiavelli, who, you may remember, wrote of princely criminality that 'if his deed accuses him, its consequences excuse him'. Even so, Kant did allow that it is morally permissible to remain silent, to withhold the truth, although you must never actually lie under any circumstances.

Kant's strong disapproval of paternalism, where governments compel their citizens to act against their will for their own good, just like well-meaning parents often treat their children, derives from his respect for human dignity, which is the only unconditional good in nature. No matter how enlightened and benevolent, paternalism is still 'the greatest despotism imaginable' because it treats rational beings as means to an end (their own wellbeing) rather than as ends in themselves. For the same reason, Kant argued that it is not the business of the state to secure the wellbeing or happiness of its citizens, contrary to the views of Aristotle (and later Martha Nussbaum), who believed that that is the ultimate end of political life. Kant saw happiness as a vague and subjective concept, unlike reason, which is objective and absolute. Political arrangements should therefore set out a stable framework of laws and institutions that allow individuals to lead a moral life and attain happiness in their own particular way, a position that has profoundly influenced late twentieth-century liberal thought, as we shall see. For Kant, a just regime will be governed by a constitution allowing the greatest possible human freedom that safeguards the freedom of others. Governments must actively safeguard individual freedom, which sometimes means forcibly removing impediments to it: for example, arresting a citizen who is threatening another and causing him not to act freely. This is what Kant called 'hindering a hindrance to freedom', which is a freedom-enhancing use of legal force. It may also justify welfare policies that support those who are unable to help themselves and whose freedom is therefore diminished, provided that it is not forced on recipients paternalistically.

It is perhaps not surprising that such a strongly moralistic outlook made Kant very wary of democracy, which he said is 'necessarily a despotism'. By 'democracy' he meant direct, participatory democracy of the kind practised in ancient Athens rather than the form of representative democracy typical today. Kant was concerned to protect individual rights and freedoms from despotism above and below, a concern he shared with nineteenth-century liberals such as John Stuart Mill and Alexis de Tocqueville. He favoured a limited constitutional state where political power is regulated by laws consistent with morality and where the civil rights of citizens are protected from the arbitrary exercise of power, including that of the 'great unthinking mass' of people. As much as Kant respected Rousseau (whose portrait alone hung in his study), he did not share his belief in democratic rule, which can too easily become tyrannical. The ideal, and safest, form of government for

Kant separates legislative from executive power and mixes authority, liberty and representative (not direct) democracy, so that only a minority of independent, propertied men (and no women) can actively participate in the making of laws, although he generously allowed that women might have the status of 'passive' citizens. In this, Kant was much closer to the conservative Hume than to the populist Rousseau.

Domestic political arrangements like these, consistent with the moral law, will always be at risk in a world of constantly warring states. So Kant proposed that all nations unite in a world federation of states committed to perpetual peace. Indeed, he claimed that everyone has a moral duty to promote this ideal as the only one compatible with the universal moral law that commands our reason. He was optimistic that, over time, world history had been moving and would continue to move in that pacific direction, however slowly – an unsurprising conclusion for someone who never left the safety and comfort of his academic perch on the Baltic.

Kant's moral idealism has proved enormously appealing to modern academic philosophers such as John Rawls, writing from his own comfortable academic perch in New England. His influential book *A Theory of Justice* helped to inspire a Kantian renaissance in the late twentieth century, as we shall see. In fact, the terms of contemporary debate in moral and political philosophy have been fundamentally shaped by Kant's writings, in the West at least. And beyond the ivory tower those writings echo very loudly today in the language of international law and political discussions about global justice and human rights. Kant's basic belief in the inherent dignity of human beings is an immensely attractive idea in a world constantly ravaged by war, exploitation and brutality.

But Kant failed to exorcize completely the ghost of Hume, whose troubling scepticism still haunts us. It is hard to share Kant's faith in reason as an infallible source of absolute moral truths, the ultimate foundations of which even he admitted were enigmatic. And many sceptics see something very parochial in his universalism and something rather sinister in his quest for moral purity. It is hard to see how any political or social system could function within the absolute ethical constraints that Kant insisted our reason commands us to obey. For example, a complete prohibition on lying, 'that admits of no expediency whatsoever', would either lead to political disaster or turn all politicians into hypocrites. Machiavelli said that, for ethical reasons, lying is an indispensable part of everyday politics, and Kant said, also for ethical reasons, that it has no place in politics ever. One held that politicians must lie constantly, the other that they must never lie. There is a lot of space between these two extremes for ethics and politics to meet.

16

Thomas Paine: The Firebrand

It is deeply ironic that Thomas Paine, the most influential and widely read advocate of revolution in his lifetime and the scourge of monarchs, came closest to being beheaded when he publicly opposed the execution of a king. Although an enthusiastic supporter of the abolition of the monarchy, Paine opposed sending the dethroned French monarch to the guillotine. Instead he proposed exiling the king to the United States, a fate worse than the guillotine for many Frenchmen, then and now. For this, and other crimes, Paine was arrested by the revolutionary government in France, where he was then living. Later, while in prison, he was among a group of inmates who were slated for execution the following day. Their cell doors were marked with chalk so their gaolers would know who had been condemned when they came in the morning to collect them for the final journey to the guillotine. Paine's door was open when it was chalked that night. So when they came for the condemned the next day, there was no mark visible on his closed cell door and he was not executed with the rest, by sheer luck. The radical revolutionaries who had ordered his death were soon overthrown by the more moderate revolutionaries supported by Paine and he was released from prison after almost a year behind bars. Paine's faith in the French Revolution, like his friend Mary Wollstonecraft's, never seriously wavered despite this near-death experience.

Like Wollstonecraft, Paine had thrown himself into the revolutionary fray in Paris, writing an inflammatory pamphlet, *The Rights of Man*, that sold even more copies than *Common Sense*, his earlier, best-selling defence of the American Revolution. And like Wollstonecraft's *Vindication of the Rights of Men*, it was a direct rebuttal of Edmund Burke's fierce attack on the Revolution, the vehemence of which had shocked Paine. He personally knew and liked Burke, who called Paine 'the great American', at least until the French Revolution. Events in France, however, pushed Paine and Burke in opposite directions, just as they divided the new political world that emerged from the Revolution into 'left' and 'right' and, in the process, gave powerful voice to two competing traditions of political thought.

Paine's influence on the political events of his times is difficult to overstate. His books and pamphlets were read by hundreds of thousands in America alone (with a population then of just 2.5 million) and did much to advance the revolutionary cause in Britain's 13 colonies in North America and in France. Even so, he always lived modestly because he refused on principle to keep the royalties his works earned. He was a popularizer of radical ideas, with a genius for expressing them in language both simple and stirring. John Adams, the future US president, wrote with only slight exaggeration that 'without the pen of Paine, the sword of Washington would have been wielded in vain'. Paine was the right man in the right place at the right time with the right message and, crucially, the right way of expressing it when he arrived in Pennsylvania from his native England in 1774.

It is remarkable that, when Paine arrived in the United States shortly before the outbreak of rebellion there, he was 37 years old, with little formal education and completely unknown, much like the penniless Rousseau when he arrived in Paris a generation earlier. *Common Sense* was published in 1776, shortly after the Revolution had started, and it exploded like a bomb, propelling Paine from obscurity to fame virtually overnight. He had brought his own radical political ideas with him from England, and these struck a deep chord with the angry mood of insurrection he found among many of the inhabitants of the 13 colonies.

Paine told his fellow colonists in blunt and impassioned terms that monarchy was an illegitimate form of governance, inherently prone to corruption and tyranny, and that they should break completely with Britain to found a new republic in which the people are sovereign. He did not flinch from violence to achieve this aim. He depicted the American Revolution as a world-historical event with global significance. The principles on which it was based – freedom, equality and democracy – are universal, which is why he supported them and why, in his view, everyone else should too. 'It was neither the place nor the people but the Cause itself that irresistibly engaged me in its support', Paine wrote. He was on the side of the rebels because their cause was 'the cause of all mankind'. This was the beginning of the idea of American 'exceptionalism', the belief that the founding of the United States was the creation of something radically new in human history with a mission to lead the world towards liberty and republicanism, an idea still popular in Paine's adopted country. He exhorted his readers to reject the past completely and 'begin the world over again' in North America by establishing a wholly new form of government and society based on reason, equality and natural rights. 'The birthday of a new world is at hand', he prophesied in 1776, predicting that, if the colonists could successfully found a new system of government embodying these principles, then 'the present generation will appear to the future as the Adam of a new world'.

At the core of Paine's assault on monarchy and aristocracy is his belief that the only legitimate basis of sovereignty is the people, a view he shared with Rousseau. Although he rejected educational and property qualifications for voting, a radical position at the time, he stopped short of advocating direct democracy or a universal franchise. Like other revolutionaries in the United States and France, he wanted the vote restricted to men; even Wollstonecraft failed to convince her friend otherwise. And Paine was a republican rather than a democrat, in the eighteenth-century understanding of those terms, meaning he supported the people's right to elect representatives rather than to participate directly in governing. He also wanted the sovereign will of the people to be limited by the principal purpose of the state: the protection of the natural rights of its members. In this Paine was closer to Locke than to Rousseau, for whom the general will was absolute. But even Paine's idea of republican representative government was too much for most of the American Founding Fathers, such as James Madison, who were terrified of mob rule and favoured extensive checks and balances in government to curb the power of the popular will. John Adams complained

THOMAS PAINE

that Paine's ideal was 'so democratical, without any restraint or even an attempt at any equilibrium or counter-poise, that it must produce confusion and every evil work'.

On the question of revolution Paine sided with Locke against Hobbes, who had argued that there can be no society without government: overthrowing the latter would destroy the former, plunging us into a war of all against all. Instead, like Locke, Paine believed that society does not depend on government for its existence. Society arises naturally to better satisfy our wants, whereas government was added later by humans to protect us from each other by 'restraining our vices'. Society is a blessing and government a 'necessary evil', he said. Society without government is not only possible but preferable when the state tramples on our natural rights. Then it becomes an unnecessary evil that should be removed, by force if necessary. For Paine, our natural rights are a 'fixed and steady principle' against which to determine the legitimacy of any government.

If governments originate in the desire to protect our natural rights, then where do those rights originate? According to Paine, their source is God, just as the US Declaration of Independence famously proclaimed: 'We hold these truths to be self-evident, that all men are created equal, that they are endowed by their Creator with certain unalienable Rights, that among these are Life, Liberty and the pursuit of Happiness'. This is also Paine's view: the moral basis of government is ultimately divine, although he denied that this involved an act of faith. He optimistically believed that knowledge of God and morality are directly discoverable by anyone who listens to 'the simple voice of reason and nature' unclouded by the emotions, prejudices and habits that Burke cherished and found so essential to social and political order.

Like most of the leading writers of the Age of Enlightenment, Paine was a deist, believing in a universal, benevolent, rational creator-God. He was severely critical of all revealed and organized religions, which are not based on either reason or evidence, for him the only true sources of knowledge. The harshness of his attacks on Christianity would later damage his reputation in the United States, to which he returned a few years before his death in 1809, when a wave of religiosity was beginning to sweep over the young country. Many denounced him as 'a filthy little atheist', as he was branded by the future US president Theodore Roosevelt because he was anti-Christian, even though Paine was as opposed to atheism as he was to fanaticism. He even helped to found a new deist Church of Theophilanthropy in France. He relied on popular eighteenth-century defences of deism, such as the argument from design (what is today called 'intelligent design'), to make his case for the existence of God. If Paine did read Hume's influential criticisms of these ideas in his *Dialogues Concerning Natural Religion*, they don't appear to have made any impression on him when he set out his defence of his moral and religious views in his book *The Age of Reason*. This is unfortunate, since he made his ethical and political principles depend on religious arguments that had already been subjected to withering criticism by Hume.

Where Hume and Paine did agree is that commerce is a major civilizing force in human history. Both optimistically believed in the power of markets, when judiciously regulated and corrected by governments, to harmonize competing interests, integrate society and promote human wellbeing.

Paine and Hume alike expected commerce to foster unity between nations as well as within them. Paine condemned the 'greedy hand of government' for 'thrusting itself into every corner and crevice of industry, and grasping the spoil of the multitude'. The irony of this from someone who, as a young man in England, had been a tax collector for King George III was not lost on Paine's enemies, who missed no opportunity to highlight his apparent hypocrisy.

Although Paine considered private property to be a God-given right that the state should protect, he also supported the state's right to confiscate it in the public interest, a stance that has given rise to questions about his consistency. He personally benefited from this when the Senate of New York granted him a small farm which had been confiscated from an exiled Loyalist, although he later complained that he should be offered something better. 'Say not that this is revenge', Paine wrote of such confiscations, 'call it rather the soft resentment of a suffering people'. He also favoured a system of taxation to limit inequalities of wealth and to fund public welfare, social insurance, free public education for the poor and pensions for the elderly, ideas whose time would not come until the twentieth century. Among the more radical public policies Paine advocated was that of giving all citizens a one-off payment of £15 when they reached the age of 21 to launch them into the world with a fighting chance of success. While he was not a socialist, or even a social democrat, Paine inspired many on the left and far left after his death with his arguments for some common provision for the welfare of citizens in need of it, funded by taxes on those who can afford it.

The case for a commercial republic that Paine presented would not have impressed either Hume or Rousseau, both of whom believed that republican virtues are incompatible with commercial society. One must choose, they believed, so Hume chose commerce and Rousseau republicanism. Looking at the United States today, it is difficult to disagree with Hume and Rousseau on this point. Commerce has been supreme for too long in the United States for the idea of a republic to seem anything but quaint now. The combination of commercialism and republicanism that Paine supported in the relatively small, predominantly rural, early American republic is not plausible today. As Rousseau saw, republics only really thrive on a small scale and in conditions of simplicity, solidarity and equality that commercial society tends to undermine. These conditions are virtually impossible to sustain in the massive, complex, globalized and increasingly unequal capitalist society that most people now inhabit in the West.

Paine's writings were so successful in his lifetime in part because he was able to connect contemporary events in America and France with a very powerful narrative of human progress and enlightenment that was immensely attractive to many ordinary people who hoped for something better. They will continue to inspire readers as long as that optimistic narrative has appeal, as it always will, to some degree. But there are many other powerful narratives competing with it, as we have seen here throughout the history of ideas.

17

Georg Wilhelm Friedrich Hegel: The Mystic

Napoleon defeated the Prussian armies in 1806 and then captured Jena, the academic home of Georg Wilhelm Friedrich Hegel. Seeing Napoleon triumphantly enter the city, the awed German philosopher was reported to have said: 'I have seen the World-Spirit today on horseback'. Hegel, who called himself a professor of World Knowledge, no less, had a philosophical imagination of unparalleled scope and ambition: he aspired to explain everything, from atomic physics to modern politics. This cosmic philosophical ambition is regarded as ludicrously overblown and pretentious by some philosophers, but as inspiring and impressive by others.

Although some contemporary 'Hegelians' have attempted to predict the future, Hegel himself insisted that philosophy is necessarily backward-looking, since we can only understand things in retrospect: 'the owl of Minerva [the Greek symbol of wisdom] takes flight only at dusk', he said. Although life must be lived prospectively, it can only be understood retrospectively. Hegel did not predict

the victory of Napoleon – let alone the 'end of history' –
but he did attempt to explain that (short-lived) victory
philosophically. According to Hegel, all of human history
reflects the action of divine mind (what he called '*Geist*'
or 'Spirit') in the pursuit of human freedom. History is
'theodicy' – that is, the story of divine justice. Individual
leaders, classes, nations and empires all come before the
judgement seat and chopping-block of history. Often the
good seem to be defeated and the evil seem to prosper.
But nothing happens by accident: every historical event
in its own way marks the progress of reason and freedom,
although this is usually only apparent in retrospect. In
biblical history, divine providence turns even the 'defeats'
of Israel into instruments of ultimate victory. Similarly,
in world history, what Hegel calls the 'cunning of reason'
ensures that even war, slavery and imperialism ultimately
serve to promote human freedom.

The French Revolution, even in its 'fury of destruction',
was necessary, says Hegel, to destroy the feudal order in
France and to liberate human personality. Every year of
his adult life, Hegel celebrated Bastille Day and toasted
the Revolution. But he also recognized the Revolution's
limitations. Inspired by purely abstract ideals of liberty,
equality and fraternity, it was purely negative and
destructive, capable only of destroying the old regime,
not of creating a new one. What history demanded was
not a counter-Revolution to undo progress and attempt to
restore the status quo ante, but a leader to consolidate the
gains of the Revolution in a stable and viable new political
order. Napoleon thus 'saved' the Revolution by defeating its
reactionary opponents. If the Revolution was a thesis and
the counter-Revolution the antithesis, then Napoleon was

a temporary synthesis, combining the legal equality of all citizens (including, for the first time, Jews) with the stability of traditional autocracy. Of course, the ultimate defeat of Napoleon is also explained by Hegel: Napoleon attempted to impose French political institutions and law upon Spain and Russia, leading to a violent assertion of national traditions in the face of French 'universalism'.

Although Hegel saw Napoleon's destruction of European autocracy as necessary, he strongly rejected both French imperialism and Prussian feudal traditionalism. Out of this deadly conflict, he saw the rise of a viable synthesis in a modern constitutional state in which the rule of law protected human equality and freedom, but within the Prussian traditions of monarchy, bureaucracy and agriculture. Hegel famously described the modern Prussian state as the march of God through history: the triumph of modern freedom in the context of traditional institutions, the victory of universal ideals in a local context.

Because Hegel offers a totalizing theory of politics, which incorporates everything from the family, morality and custom to the market, law and government, his theory is often misunderstood as somehow 'totalitarian'. Indeed, the titanic struggle on the Eastern Front in the Second World War has been described as a battle between Hitler's right-wing Hegelianism and Stalin's left-wing Hegelianism. Hitler's fascist corporatism and Stalin's Marxism do have connections, however distorted, to Hegel's thought. No doubt Hegel would describe both fascism and communism as inevitable reactions to the challenges of modern industry and mass society; he would also point out that both fascism and communism, by destroying the Prussian and Russian aristocracies, could be seen to pave the way for the success of modern social democracy. Hitler, it turns out, did inadvertently promote post-war German democracy – a great example of what Hegel called 'the cunning of reason', or the way that history realizes the goal of freedom by the most improbable strategies. Everything that seems bad really serves an ultimately good end – the expansion of reason and freedom. Hegel's philosophy of history can thus be deployed to explain anything, which leads many people to suspect that it explains nothing.

Hegel's philosophical method, called 'dialectic', is better known than any of his philosophical theories. According to Hegel, when two ideas seem to be in opposition (as thesis and antithesis), we can often reconcile them by recourse to a higher-level synthesis. How does this dialectic work in actual history? One of his favourite sets of examples comes from the contrast of the ancient Greek *polis* and the modern constitutional state. For all of its artistic, intellectual and military greatness, the ancient Greek city-state could not escape tragic conflict between the community and the individual conscience. The greatest of ancient Greek dramatic tragedies, says Hegel, is Sophocles's *Antigone*. Here the right of the community to punish traitors comes into stark conflict with the right of individual conscience. The ruler of Thebes, Creon, rightly forbids anyone to bury the body of the traitor Polynices. But Antigone claims that divine law rightly enjoins her to bury her brother, despite Creon's command. Similarly, in actual Athenian history, we see Socrates condemned by his fellow citizens for impiety and corrupting the youth; Socrates claims that he was only following the divine voice of his conscience.

According to Hegel, Antigone and Socrates must die because, within the limits of the ancient Greek *polis*, there is no way to reconcile the competing claims of the state (the thesis) and of the individual conscience (the antithesis). It is only with the rise of the universal Christian principle of the inviolability of conscience, as recognized by the modern liberal state, that these tragic conflicts can be overcome. Modern political communities, says Hegel, are objectively superior to ancient city-states precisely because they transcend these tragic conflicts by protecting both the rights of the community and the rights of individual conscience.

Whatever one thinks of Hegel's sweeping vision of history, he can help us to think through the many conflicts we see in liberal societies between individual rights and communal customs. He attacked the natural rights theorists from Hobbes to Kant for starting their political theories with individuals and their abstract rights. If we start with an individual, shorn of any social context, an 'unencumbered self', and endow him or her with an abstract set of rights to autonomy – equality, free expression and the like – then we shall create endless conflicts once we place him or her back into society. These rights are so open-ended and expansive that they make it impossible for individuals to live together. All actual communities involve limits on autonomy, equality and freedom so that people can co-exist and co-operate in families, firms, armies and polities. Indeed, Hegel attributes the failure of the French Revolution to the attempt to endow all citizens with abstract rights to liberty, equality and fraternity, which were then used to destroy all claims of existing social institutions.

Instead of starting with individuals shorn of social context and armed with abstract rights, Hegel says that we must begin with lived human communities and ethical customs. Unless our moral ideals and legal rights are embedded in social customs and habits, they will always feel alien and merely external to our conduct. Genuine natural rights must become second nature through habituation in custom. Hegel rejects the conservative appeal to prescription, custom and tradition as brute fact. What gives our social customs normative force is not merely that they are traditional but that we can see their rational purpose.

When Hegel says that 'the rational is the actual and the actual is the rational', he is not saying that 'the rational is whatever exists' or that might makes right. The rational is always the actualization of human freedom, not just what happens to exist, which may need to be swept away by revolution. The mere existence of a set of social practices is no argument for their legitimacy: habits and customs are essential for genuine social freedom, but only if they actualize rational autonomy. Hegel thus transcends and includes both Burke, defender of particular custom, and Kant, defender of universal right. Hegel proposes instead a theory of rights in context, of rights defined not as abstract principles but in the lived reality of families, corporations and states. Instead of rights of persons, we should have rights of parents, rights of workers, rights of Christians and rights of citizens. Hegel rejects both abstract universals and concrete particulars: he instead champions what he calls 'concrete universals'. Particular social customs and institutions should be understood and reformed so that we see how they embody universal rights; and abstract rights should be incarnated into particular traditions and practices. Liberals tend to see Hegel's emphasis on ethical custom as merely a rationalization of traditional mores in the name of freedom, while conservatives tend to see Hegel's emphasis on the progress of freedom as a justification for destructive and revolutionary change.

How might we think of Hegelian 'rights in context' in relation to contemporary ethical and political debates? Our debates about abortion are especially polarizing and bitter precisely because we see the brute opposition of two highly abstract individual rights: the right of a woman to autonomy and the right of the unborn child to life. The woman and the unborn child are each described as isolated individuals armed with abstract rights. Within the terms of liberal rights theory, there is no 'solution' to this conflict, only an outcome. What does this dilemma look like if we interpret rights contextually? Within the context of the relationship between a mother and her baby, we see that traditionally mothers have a customary and legal right to give up their children to adoption. What this means is that even a pregnant woman has in principle a right to separation from her unwanted baby. Unfortunately, with current technology, that separation usually requires the death of the baby, which violates the duty of parents to their children. But in the near future, it will be feasible to separate the foetus from its mother without killing it, thereby protecting the rights of both mother and unborn child. Hegel's conception of rights in context thus enables us to overcome the often tragic conflict between the rights of individuals and the relationships central to our lives. According to Hegel, we should not have to choose between rights and relationships, between individuals and communities.

18

James Madison: The Founder

After the American Revolution, the independent colonies were loosely united under the Articles of Confederation (1781). But this fledgling national government was not able to raise taxes, promote interstate trade or protect the new states from foreign aggression. Leaders from the various states agreed to organize a new and stronger national government, calling for a US Constitutional Convention in 1787.

To prepare for this upcoming convention, James Madison, a Virginia delegate, devoted himself to learning all he could about federal and republican governments. He wrote to his best friend and political ally, Thomas Jefferson – who was serving as an American delegate to the court of France – to request some treatises on ancient and modern federal republics, 'especially by Greek and Roman authors'. Jefferson scoured the bookstalls of Paris, shipping 197 books, mostly in French, to Madison in Virginia.

Madison's reputation as the 'father of the constitution of the United States' and, more generally, as the greatest theorist and practitioner of constitutional design in history, rests upon his deep learning. Unlike most great political thinkers, however, Madison combined prodigious book-learning with wide experience as a politician – making him a philosopher among statesmen and a statesman among philosophers. He followed in Jefferson's footsteps through political office from the Virginia state legislature to the Continental Congress and from Secretary of State to President of the United States. Although he lacked Jefferson's soaring rhetoric ('all men are created equal'), Madison tempered Jeffersonian ideals of popular government with both greater realism about human nature and keener insights about institutional dynamics. Jefferson, for example, wanted each generation to write its own constitution. What does rule of the people mean if the people are governed by the dead? Madison insisted, by contrast, that healthy democratic politics required a fixed framework of basic law. Changing the constitution frequently would be like changing the rules of a game in the middle of play, undermining the fairness of democratic competition for power. Madison's contributions to *The Federalist Papers* – a collection of essays explaining and defending the proposed new constitution – are what make it America's greatest contribution to the history of political thought.

At the College of New Jersey (now Princeton University), the young Madison acquired an Augustinian pessimism about human nature from his teacher John Witherspoon, a Calvinist Christian from Scotland. Augustine, you will recall, has been called the first political realist because of his view of radical human evil – a tendency to selfishness that may be tempered but never eliminated by upbringing or education. Because of this radical human evil, 'power tends to corrupt, and absolute power corrupts absolutely', in the later words of Lord Acton. What this means is that no set of rulers – no matter how 'virtuous' – can be entrusted with plenary political power. Echoing Augustine, Madison famously said: 'If men were angels, no government would be necessary'. Appraising Madison's institutional machinery for controlling the arbitrary exercise of power, Immanuel Kant claimed that a well-designed constitution could work even with a 'race of devils'. Madison would not go that far. He insisted that a sufficient lack of civic virtue among citizens and politicians would undermine any constitutional arrangement.

Having just rejected the tyranny of the British Crown and Parliament, Madison feared that Americans would now become tyrannized by their fellow citizens. Already, in the Confederated States, he had witnessed large numbers of debtors expropriating the wealth of the smaller number of creditors. Much worse, of course, was the long-term tyranny of white majorities over racial minorities. The fundamental challenge for Madison throughout his life was to figure out how to combine popular government with individual liberty: how to empower democratic majorities without tyrannizing minorities. European history seemed to suggest that unpopular minorities, such as Jews, were often protected better by monarchs than by popular assemblies.

It is often said that Madison favoured republican government over democratic government, but it would be more accurate to say that he favoured a democratic republic. He often disparaged what he called 'pure' democracy, meaning ancient direct democracy, in which every citizen could vote on every issue. Passions among citizens, he thought, would lead to tyrannical assemblies: 'Even if every ancient Athenian were a Socrates, every Athenian assembly would be a mob'. Madison favoured the practice of representation in which a few men would govern on behalf of the others, so that the raw passions of the people might be moderated by the deliberation of their representatives. Many republics in history were aristocratic; Madison insisted upon a democratic republic. The ancient world gave us models of direct democracy that were not representative; medieval Europe gave us models of representative governments that were not democratic. Madison pioneered the development of a truly representative democracy, combining ancient and medieval political ideals.

Madison's genius as a political thinker is evident in how he overturns some basic assumptions of traditional political thought and practice. One basic axiom of all ancient and medieval politics was the idea that a community could not be politically united unless it was religiously united. Virtually all governments in human history have claimed the right to enforce religious orthodoxy in the name of political unity. Jefferson and Madison rejected this traditional assumption when they enacted Virginia's statute of religious liberty, which became the model for the First Amendment protections of free exercise of religion in the US Constitution. Madison argued that a state-established church corrupted both the state and religion and that religious pluralism made for better churches and better governments. The enforcement of religious orthodoxy, he insisted, does not prevent but actually creates political conflict. As it turned out, American Christianity spread more rapidly under religious liberty than under any state-established Christian church.

A second basic axiom of traditional political theory was that a democratic polity must be small and homogeneous. Ancient democracies, after all, were tiny city-states. As the

Roman republic became a large empire, the Roman people lost their political liberties. Champions of states' rights in the US, who opposed Madison's new national government, insisted that representatives would be accountable to the people only in small states. But the history of small republics, ancient and modern, Madison argued, proves that they all founder upon factional conflict. Indeed, the smaller the polity, the more likely it is to devolve into two warring blocks: rich versus poor, creditors versus debtors, Catholic versus Protestant. Given the diversity of human temperaments and circumstances, no free society will ever reach spontaneous unanimity. Faction and division cannot be suppressed.

The solution to the mortal danger of warring factions is, paradoxically, the multiplication of factions. David Hume had already noted that religious liberty fares best where there are many religious sects, preventing any one sect from oppressing the others. Madison generalized this insight by arguing that a large and diverse polity will contain so many degrees and kinds of property, so many religions, so many geographical and cultural identities, that no single divide will threaten civil war. In a large and geographically diverse nation, said Madison, each citizen will have many identities: for example, poor, Catholic, urban, northern and white. Instead of exhorting citizens to work for the common good, Madison accepts the reality of parochial self-interest. Factions are inevitable; safety is found in the multiplicity of cross-cutting groups. Before Madison, no one had argued that a large democratic republic was more viable than a small one.

A third basic axiom of traditional political thought is that every government must have a sovereign authority. In

European polities, the king is sovereign or the parliament is sovereign or the 'king-in-parliament' is sovereign. What is sovereignty? Sovereign authority is final and cannot be challenged; sovereign authority is indivisible, to avoid impasse; sovereign power cannot be legally limited, because whatever limits sovereignty is itself sovereign. Although Madison would argue that in the US 'the people' are sovereign, the genius of his constitutional design is that sovereignty is located everywhere – and nowhere. First, he divided the national government from the governments of the several states. Is the national government sovereign, or are the state governments sovereign? The answer is 'yes' to both. As for the national and state governments, these are then internally divided into executive, legislative and judicial branches, each with its own powers to check and balance the other branches. It makes no sense even to ask which branch of government is sovereign. Not even the whole government is sovereign, since the people can organize state constitutional conventions to abolish state or national governments.

What if two or more branches of government collude to usurp power? Madison was well aware that mere constitutional provisions, or what he disparaged as 'parchment barriers', could not stop ambitious politicians from ignoring legal niceties. He argued that the institutional separation of offices would lead to salutary conflict among office-holders, so that 'ambition must be made to counteract ambition'. Politicians would jealously protect the powers and prerogatives of their branch of government against other branches, not from high-minded loyalty to the constitution but merely to protect their own power base. According to Madison's political psychology, politicians identify with their offices, so that 'where you stand depends upon where you sit'. Instead of exhorting politicians to defend the constitution, he relies upon their conflicting ambitions to check their power. He takes human beings as they are, not as they might be.

Madison is often called the father of the US Constitution because of his intellectual leadership of the Constitutional Convention of 1787. Yet his preferred 'Virginia Plan' – which erected a much stronger national government with power of veto over all legislation by individual states – was defeated. Madison was much more directly responsible for drafting the first ten amendments of the Constitution, known as the Bill of Rights – the most influential statement of basic liberties in world history. They are Madison's supreme political achievement.

Madison was fully aware of the hypocrisy of being a champion of human rights while also owning slaves. He never wavered from his condemnation of slavery as a moral evil but also never attempted to abolish it. As a Virginian, he fully understood that the southern states would never join a Union at the cost of surrendering slavery. Jefferson and Madison were both targets of the bitter reproach against American revolutionaries by the English writer Samuel Johnson: 'How is it that we hear the loudest yelps for liberty among the drivers of negroes?'

Madison's overriding aim in constitutional design was to avoid the dangers of tyranny – especially of the majority. His maxim was 'divide and govern': first, by enlarging the republic and dividing society into many cross-cutting factions so that no stable majority can oppress a minority; second, by dividing sovereignty between national and state governments; third, by dividing governments internally into branches so that competition among politicians prevents any conspiracy against the people. The danger of this dispersal of sovereignty is that it can often lead to an impasse: since no branch has full power, each often simply vetoes the agenda of the other branches. Also, since no branch of government is sovereign, voters often do not know whom to credit or blame. The dispersal of sovereignty usually entails the dispersal of accountability. Ever since Woodrow Wilson (in office 1913–21), American progressives have argued that Madison's constitution so weakens the national government that reform of US society is almost always stymied by organized special interests.

Madison's is the only modern constitution in the world that makes no provision for political parties. Yet without parties there could be no stable co-operation among branches and thus no capacity to govern. At the same time, parties undermine the tendency of each branch to check the other branches: where one party controls two or more branches of government, checks and balances are weakened. Political parties are thus necessary for governing while they also undermine Madison's carefully calibrated controls on the exercise of power.

Ever since Madison, political scientists and economists have devised increasingly complex and subtle institutional incentives and constraints designed to 'nudge' people to do the right thing. For example, today we structure choices to be an organ donor or to save money for retirement by making the 'virtuous' choice the default option. We provide financial incentives to encourage companies to stop polluting or to offer health insurance to their employees. Like Madison, we carefully structure our institutions so that people make the 'right' choice for the wrong reasons.

Meanwhile, unlike Madison, we have largely abandoned the whole language of moral character and civic virtue. The use of public office for subsequent private enrichment, once castigated as corrupt, is now almost universally accepted. We know from history and from contemporary politics that no constitutional arrangement – no matter how carefully designed – can control politicians who lack essential civic virtues.

19

Alexis de Tocqueville: The Prophet

The French writer Alexis de Tocqueville never once attended a New England town meeting, despite travelling throughout Massachusetts and Connecticut in the autumn of 1831. Yet he begins his classic book *Democracy in America* by effusively praising the New England town meeting as the world's best example of democratic virtue in action. Instead of passively waiting for the state or national government to solve their local problems, these sturdy, independent farmers and tradesmen would come together periodically to discuss, debate and decide the local issues before them – raising money, allocating funds and building roads or schools. Tocqueville concedes that American local government is often inept – but that, he says, doesn't matter: American towns possess the supreme virtue of teaching citizens how to make honourable use of their freedom by governing themselves. Tocqueville's focus on town meetings in his study of American democracy is puzzling, since those meetings resemble ancient Greek direct democracy more than modern American representative democracy. But Tocqueville was writing to instruct his fellow Frenchmen, not the Americans.

As a French aristocrat who embraced the rise of democracy, Tocqueville hoped that some of the robust self-sufficiency of his feudal ancestors might inform the character of modern democratic citizens. In the distant European past, before the rise of the modern state, feudal nobles convened to govern their common affairs, each man respecting the freedom and independence of his peers. Tocqueville wanted every democratic citizen to act with the civic virtue of these idealized nobles: an aristocracy of everyone. He claimed that emerging democratic legal and moral equality is the irresistible will of God – our own choices will decide only if we have equality of freedom or equality of servitude, a society of independent citizens or a society of lackeys. Tocqueville foresaw two primary threats to his beloved political liberty: governmental centralization and market consumerism, both of which cause people to withdraw from the demands of civic virtue into a private life of quiet servitude. Like an Old Testament prophet, he not only claimed to see the will of God in the rise of democratic equality but also warned us of a possible future in which the democratic 'herd' fattens itself on private luxuries while being shepherded by remote powers – a vision of what he called a 'soft despotism' eerily applicable to both twentieth-century communism and, perhaps, to twenty-first-century capitalism.

What enabled Tocqueville to be a democrat among aristocrats? He lived after the death of French aristocracy but before the birth of French democracy. His life's mission was to warn aristocrats that democracy was inevitable and to warn democrats that political liberty was not inevitable. No prophet is honoured in his own country, and Tocqueville was never embraced by either French aristocrats or democrats; his estrangement from French politics made possible his vocation as a writer. Only an aristocrat could write so brilliantly of democracy, and only a Frenchman (or foreigner) could write so brilliantly of America.

Tocqueville lived in the shadow of the French Revolution of 1789, in which many of his relatives, and very nearly his parents, were executed. His contemporaries were deeply divided over the justice of this epochal event, but all agreed that it represented a radical break with feudal monarchy. Tocqueville alone insisted that the Revolution merely removed the debris of a feudal order already destroyed by monarchs since King Louis XIV. French feudalism was bitterly hated only after it had largely ceased to exist: by the eighteenth century, French nobles possessed many privileges but no real power; they had all the rewards of governing without having to govern. Ambitious monarchs during the previous two centuries had monopolized all political power in Paris. The revolutionaries of 1789 and then Napoleon merely perfected the centralizing administration pioneered by the absolute monarchs, bypassing the nobles and governing the people directly.

What caused the Revolution? Tocqueville journeyed to the United States to seek American answers (and solutions) to French questions. Just as the key to American democracy is found in local government, so too is the key to the French Revolution. Under medieval and early modern feudalism, peasants provided labour and taxes to local nobles in return for being governed by them. But, by the eighteenth century, peasants found themselves being governed by functionaries from Paris – yet still being taxed to support their useless local nobles, many of whom had decamped to Versailles. This absurdity could not last, and indeed did not.

The events of 1789 were merely the violent culmination of a quiet political, economic and social revolution that had already transformed local French life. By studying local government, Tocqueville discerned the hidden secrets of both American and French politics.

It always makes sense to look at local government, says Tocqueville, because the habits of the heart, which are the basis of all politics, are formed by people's everyday experiences. For most, concepts such as democracy or constitutionalism are vague abstractions, and places such as Washington DC or Paris are like foreign lands. Americans acquired their democratic habits not from schools or books but from serving on parish councils, town committees and local juries. Civic virtues are a set of habits acquired from co-operating with one's neighbours, learning to tolerate differences and reaching solutions to common problems. According to Tocqueville, Americans first organized townships, then states and, finally, the national government. What this means is that Americans instinctively think of all levels of government by analogy to their familiar towns. Tocqueville would have agreed with G. K. Chesterton that democracy is like blowing one's nose: even if done badly, one should do it for oneself.

Although Tocqueville was a passionate advocate for the virtues of local government, this does not imply that he was a supporter of states' rights. According to him, state governments were almost as remote from everyday life as the national government. Tocqueville endorsed the Federalist or Hamiltonian (named after Alexander Hamilton) interpretation of the US Constitution, defending a strong national government; he rejected the Republican or Jeffersonian defence of state sovereignty. Tocqueville, with his usual prescience, worried that the power of the states to ignore the mandates of the national government threatened the survival of the Union, as indeed it did during the later Civil War. Tocqueville comments that he frequently heard Americans denounce the tyranny of the national government – without any plausible evidence. Indeed, according to Tocqueville, the state governments were in fact the primary threat to liberty.

A burning French question, for which Tocqueville sought an American answer, was the relation of Christianity to politics. The Catholic Church in France had for centuries allied itself with the monarchy. As a consequence, when the monarchy was pulled down in 1792, the Church was buried in the ruins. After the Revolution, both the French right and left largely agreed on one axiom: Catholicism is royalist and anti-democratic; democratic equality and liberty are secular, non-Christian ideals. Tocqueville was never more passionate or resolute than in his insistence, to the contrary, that modern democracy is a Christian ideal and that Jesus came to earth to proclaim the equality of every human being. This was also a burning personal question for Tocqueville, who lost his Catholic faith but not his love for Christianity.

Ancient democracy, says Tocqueville, was based on slavery, class privilege and patriarchy. Even Plato and Aristotle explicitly endorsed radical human inequality. The ideals of universal human equality, rights and liberty were the gift of Christianity. He chided Christian theologians and preachers for not developing a Christian ethics of citizenship. Royalists, monarchists, democrats, socialists and anarchists alike were all convinced that Christianity was fundamentally opposed to modern democracy. Tocqueville, anticipating Nietzsche, argued that Christianity, whatever its current institutional corruption, is actually the origin of our democratic ideals. More importantly still, said Tocqueville, Christianity is necessary for the survival of democratic civic virtues.

While visiting the United States, Tocqueville was struck by two things: first, the separation of church and state (even though, at the time of his visit, several American states still had established churches); second, that despite this separation – or rather, because of it – the Christian religion was 'the foremost of American political institutions'. How could a private religion be the foremost of *political* institutions? We must remember that politics stems from 'habits of the heart' and Americans were shaped more profoundly by their churches than by any other institution. Among the Puritans who settled New England, for example, all ministers were elected by their congregations; even Catholic bishops in America were originally elected by their priests. American churches, in short, were democratic even before American governments. Without religion, said Tocqueville, Americans would become utterly absorbed in selfish individualism, especially the quest for material wealth. The habits of the heart, formed not so much by Christian teaching as by participation in Christian communities, were what led Americans to civic virtues. Social scientists today, inspired by Tocqueville, have indeed discovered a strong relationship between church attendance (in whatever religion) and many measures of civic virtue.

The longer Tocqueville studied American democracy, the more pessimistic he became. The most fundamental source of his pessimism centred upon the relations among blacks, Indians and whites. Like all enlightened French liberals, Tocqueville was horrified by American slavery – not only by the appalling degradation of the slaves but also by the corruption of the masters. He argued that slavery dishonoured labour, making southern whites lazy, ignorant and proud. While sailing down the Ohio River, Tocqueville claimed that the farms on the free Ohio side were orderly and industrious compared with the slovenly shambles on the slave-holding Kentucky side of the river. Ancient slavery, he observed, bound the body but not the mind; American racial slavery, by contrast, degraded both the body and the mind of the slave, who thought of himself as naturally inferior. The crimes against blacks, said Tocqueville, cried out for vengeance; he saw race war in the US as more likely than peaceful co-existence.

Arriving in the US just after the Indian Removal Act of 1830, Tocqueville saw no future for American Indians apart from extermination by the relentlessly greedy and violent white settlers. He said that the proud Indian warriors, who preferred death to servitude, reminded him of his own noble ancestors, who were of the military aristocracy. Nothing reveals more about Tocqueville's own aristocratic character than his deep admiration for the courage and stoicism of American Indian warriors in the face of total destruction.

Democratic culture, said Tocqueville, is thoroughly practical, materialistic and empirical. That is why, he added, Americans excel in the development of new technologies – so long as they are profitable in the short term. Common sense would seem to dictate that a pragmatic American culture requires a pragmatic and vocational American schooling – and, indeed, American schooling has generally been robustly practical. As usual, Tocqueville rejected the common sense of his contemporaries and insisted that what pragmatic American democrats really needed was a useless aristocratic schooling in classical languages and literature, philosophy, fine arts and music. Schools should aim to ennoble democratic culture by enticing students to raise their hearts and minds to the love of pure truth, noble moral ideals and sheer beauty. Without such an education, democracy would sink into a narrow vocationalism – ultimately undermining the progress of the arts and sciences so cherished by Americans. Yes, practical, can-do Americans need above all to study ballet.

Today, there is widespread dismay about the perceived lack of civic virtue in advanced democracies. Because real political power is now located in distant national capitols or even in international organizations, most citizens have become mere spectators – and politics itself a sorry spectacle of vulgar tribal conflict amid cynical self-dealing. As a consequence, many citizens in America and in Europe are looking to their schools to teach the civic virtue so lacking in public life. Can civic virtue be taught in schools? Tocqueville thought not: 'Local institutions are to liberty what elementary schools are to knowledge; they bring it within the reach of the people'. The virtues of political liberty must be learned by active participation in local churches, organizations and governments. Civic virtues are ultimately habits of the heart, not lessons of the mind. But if our local institutions have been hollowed out by internet consumerism and political centralization, where might citizens acquire the right habits of the heart?

20

John Stuart Mill: The Individualist

For 35 years (over half his life) John Stuart Mill worked as a civil servant in the London headquarters of the British East India Company, a private venture with a royal charter that administered British trade in the Far East and effectively ruled India. When he retired from the company, he held the senior post of Examiner that his father, James Mill, had held before him. Needless to say, neither Mill ever set foot in the country they helped to administer from London for so many decades. Nor, for that matter, is there any evidence that either of them ever actually met an Indian. Although a liberal democrat and a self-styled 'radical', Mill believed despotism 'a legitimate mode of government in dealing with barbarians', which included the native population of India, in his view. In that he was a man of his times. He believed that all people are inherently able to ascend to the level of 'civilization', as Britain had, more or less. (Mill, who is buried in France, was that most unnatural of beings, an English Francophile.) Although he had no time for the biological theories of race that were becoming increasingly popular across Europe in the second half of the nineteenth century, Mill was sure that different societies sit on different rungs of the ladder of human progress, and that 'backward states of society' should not enjoy the kinds of individual freedoms and democratic rights typically found in the most 'advanced' states until they have reached the same high level of development. He hoped and expected most peoples to reach this stage of advancement eventually, although he never believed that it would be easy or inevitable in any case. Despotism is legitimate only if it is enlightened, and in the progressive interests of those over whom it is wielded, a position Mill shared with Karl Marx, who wrote that 'England has to fulfil a double mission in India: one destructive, the other regenerating the annihilation of old Asiatic society, and then laying the material foundations of Western society in Asia.'

If Mill was a man of his times on matters of colonialism, he was well ahead of them in other ways. He was the greatest nineteenth-century theorist and advocate of women's equality – a very unpopular position at the time that made him many enemies in Victorian Britain. He was the first politician in the United Kingdom to include extending the vote to women on a political platform when he ran for Parliament, where he campaigned for women's suffrage. As a Member of Parliament (for just three years) Mill presented the first mass women's suffrage petition to the House of Commons and proposed an amendment to include women in the 1867 Reform Bill that extended voting rights for most propertied men. (The bill passed, but his amendment was defeated.) It was not for another half a century that Britain was ready for such change. He wrote a pioneering feminist book, *On the Subjection of Women*, which sets out the case for treating women and men equally in all respects. In it, Mill argues that the exclusion of women from public life and the professions is 'one of the chief hindrances to human improvement'. In this, and in many other ways, he was strongly influenced by his wife, Harriett Taylor, the author of an influential essay on 'The Enfranchisement of Women'. In his *Autobiography*, Mill describes his personal and intellectual debt to her as 'almost infinite' and claims that all of his published writings were 'joint productions' with his wife, even though her name appears on none of them. Even Mill's feminism had its limits, it seems.

Mill's greatest legacy is not his long career as an imperial civil servant or his short career as a politician. He is remembered now for his writings, foremost of which is his essay *On Liberty* (1859), perhaps the most famous and influential defence of individual freedom ever written. It was the work he was most proud of and correctly predicted would 'survive longer than anything else that I have written'.

What most concerned Mill in his own time was the 'tyranny of the prevailing opinion and feeling' over exceptional individuals, a concern he shared with other nineteenth-century liberals such as his friend Alexis de Tocqueville, who worried above all about threats to freedom from social pressure and conformity. Mill was convinced that the rise of mass society risked crushing individuality and smothering dissent, the consequence of which would be to slow or even stop human advancement, which depends on the free expression of ideas and 'experiments in living'.

Politically, Mill was a classical liberal who believed that the best means to promote human wellbeing is a general policy of allowing the greatest possible scope for individual liberty consistent with the liberty of others. Ethically, he was a utilitarian, like his father. Indeed, he called it his 'religion'. Unlike most liberals, the Mills rejected any doctrine of natural rights. As we have seen, John Locke was the founder of Anglo-American liberalism who declared that every person was born possessing a natural right to life, liberty and property; Thomas Jefferson famously endorsed Lockean natural rights in the American Declaration of Independence. Mill set himself the challenge of defending individual liberty and equality of the sexes without recourse to any doctrine of natural rights to freedom or equality or, like Paine, by invoking God. The foundation of his defence ultimately lies in the utility of those causes, their capacity to promote human wellbeing, something strictly forbidden by Kant, who called such an approach the 'euthanasia of all morality'.

According to Mill, if each of us is left free to pursue our 'own good in our own way', we are more likely to find the truth, and the truth is the best way to improve overall human wellbeing in the long run. Society should be configured to allow 'persons of genius' (male and female) the widest freedom to expand their minds, express their ideas and permit the free development of their individuality. It is only in such an atmosphere that exceptional individual talents can flourish and drive progress, dragging the whole of society with them on an upward march to civilization. Mill was keenly aware of just how rare and difficult it is to sustain the conditions in which genius can thrive. He thought that our mental powers are like muscles that weaken unless they are used regularly and vigorously. Censorship inhibits the exercise of our critical, deliberative faculties, which easily become flabby and dull. Instead, a climate should be fostered in which we are 'forever stimulating each other to increased exercise of their higher faculties' through open debate and the free exchange of ideas and opinions.

Like Kant, Mill strongly opposed paternalism – forcing people to do things for their own good – which amounts to treating adults like children. Instead, he favoured a policy of *laissez-faire*, leaving people alone to find the form of life that suits each person in their own unique way. This precept applies only to those who are in the 'maturity of their faculties', which does not include children or 'barbarians'. Paternalism is appropriate for the latter, and only until they become civilized adults capable of choosing for themselves, anticipating the consequences of their actions and accepting responsibility for them. Otherwise, individuals should be left alone, provided they leave others alone.

Since humans are fallible creatures, according to Mill, we are easily prone to error in our beliefs. It is therefore crucial to allow opinions to be expressed openly so that, in the uninhibited clash of ideas, beliefs can be tested to see how they hold up under scrutiny. Mill did not naïvely assume that the truth would necessarily prevail in this contest, but he believed it far more likely that truth would emerge under such conditions than when beliefs were dogmatically shielded from examination and criticism. Anyone is potentially wrong, so no beliefs should be treated as sacrosanct and placed beyond doubt. Human progress depends on the freedom to criticize and question. This was the main lesson and inspiration that Mill drew from the life and death of Socrates, whom he revered as a symbol of the heroic free-thinker standing up to the tyranny of the majority, for which he paid the ultimate price.

Mill was no anarchist. Like Kant, he favoured freedom within limits that must sometimes be enforced by the state. People should be free to exercise their liberty only up to the point where they cause harm to others. The only purpose, he declares in *On Liberty*, 'for which power can be rightfully exercised over any member of a civilized community, against his will, is to prevent harm to others'. As an opponent of paternalism, Mill did not believe that the state should act to prevent adults from harming themselves. So, our laws requiring the wearing of seat belts, for example, should have no place in a liberal state as Mill conceived of it. It is better to leave people to make mistakes and learn from them than to intervene to prevent self-harm.

Mill was a democrat who voted for the extension of the franchise in 1867 when he was a Member of Parliament. At the same time, he shared his friend Tocqueville's anxieties about the dominance of the poorly educated majority over the well-educated few. Therefore, he advocated a system of 'plural voting' in which every adult who could read, write and do basic arithmetic would get at least one vote, but those with a better education and possessing 'mental superiority' would get more votes, 'as a counterpoise to the numerical weight of the least educated class'. It was very common in the nineteenth century to find support for such schemes, to limit what many saw as the brute power of democratic majorities. Like most liberals, Mill was a nervous democrat, and no populist. He wished to elevate the electorate as well as expand it. As a liberal who valued individual freedom, he saw the danger that the majority poses to minorities, and proposed his system of weighting votes as a means of balancing quantity with quality, as he saw it. He also favoured representative, not direct, democracy, and agreed with Burke's case for elected representatives to be trustees of their constituents rather than their delegates. In his *Autobiography*, Mill recounts that he bluntly told local supporters who had asked him to stand for Parliament that, 'if elected, I could not undertake to give any of my time and labour to their local interests'. He even planned to remain in France during the election campaign, although he eventually gave in to pressure to face the voters. He boasted during the campaign that he had written in a pamphlet that the working classes are 'generally liars', a statement that made its way on to a placard used in the election, which he won, to his astonishment, although he stopped just short of demanding a recount when he was unexpectedly and improbably declared the winner.

Today, the value and limits of free speech are being tested and debated to a greater degree than they have been for many decades. Advances in communications technology have made the world a 'global village' where ideas and images are instantly transmitted across the planet, thereby increasing the possibility for offence and misunderstanding exponentially. This has led to calls for limits on freedom of expression. The controversies stirred by these clashes remind us that other values, such as social harmony, tolerance and respect, compete with liberty, which even Mill insisted should not be absolute. The belief in the supremacy of free expression is not self-evident to most of the world, which is not liberal. In this context, Mill's celebrated essay is perhaps needed more than ever to make the case for liberty as the highest political value in the West, and perhaps the one most likely to promote human wellbeing. Moreover, his concerns about popular democracy, long dismissed as mere snobbery, are finding a new audience among those alarmed by the rise of populism and the electoral success of parties and politicians who see liberalism itself as the problem rather than the solution to the ills of our age.

21

Karl Marx: The Revolutionary

When Karl Marx arrived in London from France as a penniless exile in 1849, he moved to a dingy little two-room flat at 28 Dean Street, a former brothel and now a fashionable restaurant in Soho, then one of the most run-down parts of the crowded, polluted city, where he lived on the brink of destitution for six years with his young family. Although he and Mill cohabited in the same city for 24 years, they lived a world apart and never met. Marx knew about Mill and read his work, but Mill had never even heard of Marx, who was an obscure German revolutionary virtually unknown in Britain in his lifetime.

Marx was saved from abject poverty only by the generosity of his wealthy German friend and patron Friedrich Engels, whose family owned textile mills in Manchester. Even so, Marx was unable to prevent the early deaths of three of his children in their squalid, cramped new home. When his infant daughter Franziska died, Marx had to borrow money to hire an undertaker to bury her. His prospects for making a living in the London of Charles Dickens were severely limited by his imperfect command of English, which he never entirely mastered, despite spending most of his life in Britain.

Like Rousseau, who had lived briefly in exile in England a century before, Marx was no Anglophile and expressed no gratitude towards his adopted country for providing him with refuge from persecution on the Continent, where the authorities had hounded him out for his radical opinions. The impecunious Marx rarely left London after moving there and never visited an English factory, despite being an analyst of industrial capitalism, a champion of workers' interests and an advocate of proletarian revolution: revolution by and for working men and women. Marx's own background was thoroughly bourgeois, not working-class. His knowledge of the plight of working people and of the laws and effects of capitalism, as he saw them, was derived almost entirely from written accounts (by government inspectors, for example), which he voraciously consumed on his daily trips to the reading room of the British Museum, a short walk away from the two 'evil, frightful rooms' where he lived with his family and housekeeper. Indeed, he spent so many hours sitting on the hard, uncushioned chairs at the museum that he developed boils on his posterior. He blamed his anger at the bourgeoisie on the pain and discomfort caused by these uncomfortable seats. 'I hope the bourgeoisie will remember my carbuncles until their dying day', he fumed to Engels. 'What swine they are!'

Marx's studies were of early, unregulated industrial capitalism in Britain, France and Germany, a very raw and brutal form of production before the twentieth-century creation of the welfare state and enactment of labour laws and regulations to soften its excesses and protect the most vulnerable. It was described most vividly and movingly in literature by Charles Dickens, 'whose graphic and eloquent pages have issued to the world more political and social truths than have been uttered by all the professional politicians, publicists and moralists put together', Marx wrote admiringly of the great Victorian novelist. He was convinced that capitalism must inevitably self-destruct, owing to the violent booms and busts of its business cycles and the increasingly barbaric condition of the working poor. He had carefully, if selectively, analysed its inner workings in books, reports and newspapers, and concluded that it was doomed to collapse under the weight of its own internal contradictions, which made it inherently and increasingly unstable. This fate cannot be avoided, he believed. Like all class-based economic systems, capitalism rests, according to Marx, on the pitiless exploitation of the poor and powerless by the rich and powerful, and all such systems are destined to fail eventually when the lives of the impoverished majority become unbearable. That is why he said the bourgeoisie, mad with greed, are their own grave-diggers. Only after such a fall, he confidently predicted, can the positive work of establishing a communist society begin, a society free of classes, exploitation and violence.

For Marx, what he called the 'bourgeoisie', the ruling class in capitalism that owns and controls the 'means of production' (factories, money and resources), exploits the working class (the proletariat), whose sole 'possession' is their own physical ability to work (their 'labour power'). Workers are free in principle to sell this power to the bourgeoisie in return for the best wage they can get, which in the vast majority of cases is barely enough to live on. Most then toil long and hard to produce goods that are owned and sold by others for their profit. It is a system of pure exploitation in which the vast majority are doomed to live desperate lives, while the privileged few enjoy conspicuous wealth and hoard all power. How do capitalists ensure that wages stay low? By creating a 'reserve army of the unemployed' ready to replace any worker who seeks higher wages. Over time, the rich get richer and the poor get poorer until the system explodes in revolutionary violence, Marx believed.

Marx argued that capitalists pretend to support competition but do everything they can to prevent it, since competition forces down prices and therefore profits. Even the classical economist Adam Smith, an admirer and defender of commercial society, had noted that whenever businessmen get together they conspire to create monopolies and cartels to drive out smaller firms ruthlessly. In addition, the relentless capitalist pressure to force down wages to inhuman levels to keep profits high is self-defeating in the long term, as workers cannot afford to buy the very goods they produce, causing a 'crisis of overproduction' that dooms capitalism. There are just too many goods chasing too few consumers, an unsustainable position over the long term.

In 1848, when a wave of uprisings swept across Europe, Marx thought that this might be the beginning of the end of capitalism, which he had predicted must eventually come. When it turned out to be a false dawn, he decided to wait for the inevitable revolution in the safe haven of London, which had a relatively relaxed attitude towards radicals and agitators, such as the members of the Communist League, whose headquarters was there and which had commissioned Marx and Engels to write their famous *Communist Manifesto*. After the League was disbanded,

Marx became an active and prominent member of the International Workingmen's Association, to whose General Council he was elected. In that role, he was one of the leaders of the international communist movement, and was regarded as its leading intellectual light. Even so, when he died in London in 1883, Marx was virtually unknown in England. He wrote exclusively in German, and only his *Communist Manifesto* had been translated into English in his lifetime. By the middle of the 1860s virtually nothing that he had written was any longer in print. Karl Marx died in relative obscurity in exile, waiting for the revolution that he was convinced must one day come. When it finally came, three decades later, it was in a place where he had never expected it: Russia.

Like Augustine and Hobbes, Marx saw the state entirely negatively. Government, he wrote, is just a weapon of the ruling class to keep the rest in line. He considered political power as merely 'the organized power of one class for oppressing another'. The state is never really fair or just, despite its façade of formally impartial laws and procedures. It always acts in the interests of the dominant class, since that is its sole purpose, and never for the general good. Although the state relies heavily (and often brutally) on force to repress dissent and maintain order, capitalism also plays with our minds, distorting our perception of the awful reality in which most live under capitalism through ideology, which includes religion. This is necessary because the conditions in which the majority live and work are so oppressive and exploitative that, if they were viewed accurately, they would provoke spontaneous rebellions. Ideology acts like a camera obscura, turning our understanding of reality on its head so that we accept our exploitation as legitimate. For example, workers in capitalism are told that they are 'free' agents who may contract out their labour to the highest bidder for a wage. This fiction acts to reconcile them to what is really just a form of mass wage slavery, in which workers have no effective power to negotiate better conditions and higher wages. That is why Marx believed that capitalism is doomed since, while the rich continue to add to their own wealth and power, the condition of the vast majority gradually declines.

Marx believed that, after the inevitable revolution and with the abolition of class society, the state will eventually become unnecessary. But first there must be a transition period when the bourgeois state is seized by the proletariat after the fall of capitalism and used to crush the remnants of the old system to secure the total victory of the workers. Marx called this temporary stage on the road to communism the 'dictatorship of the proletariat', where the bourgeois state, now in the hands of the working class, forcibly dismantles the system of private property established under capitalism and classes disappear. The Soviet Union remained stuck in this stage for seven decades, waiting for the rest of the capitalist world to collapse so that it could move on to the next stage, communism. Instead, it was the Soviet Union that collapsed, and Russia reverted to capitalism.

In Marx's theory, when this task of dismantling the capitalist system is complete, class conflict will cease, since classes will no longer exist. For him, competition, selfishness, violence and fraud are essential features of all class-based societies but are not inherent in our nature. So, under communism, which is classless, these evils will disappear and our spontaneously co-operative nature can finally emerge, making the coercive state redundant;

it simply 'withers away', in Friedrich Engels' words, as it is no longer needed. All of the goods and resources that are produced and distributed under communism will be allocated according to need, so that communist society works for all and everyone's needs are equally satisfied. Citizens don't keep what they make as their own private property, which was abolished with capitalism. Nor, under communism, would they want to.

Beyond these very sketchy and limited ideas about communism, Marx said surprisingly little about the shape of things to come following the demise of capitalism, in stark contrast to the many long, turgid volumes that he wrote explaining the inner workings of the capitalist system in immense detail, particularly the massive, unfinished multivolume work *Capital*. This reticence about communism was no accident: Marx claimed that 'anyone who writes about the future is a reactionary'. He derided utopian socialists for merely recreating medieval communalism when writing about the future. Marx wanted to leave the post-capitalist future open to its own unforeseeable developments. He was primarily an analyst and critic of early industrial capitalism with relatively little to say about the possible future of communist society, whose character he left deliberately vague.

The history and eventual collapse of the Soviet Union, the world's first officially Marxist state, has done much to discredit Marx's ideas, just as the Jacobin appropriation of Rousseau's thought during the French Revolution tarnished his reputation in the eyes of many. Likewise, the Nazi embrace of the German thinker Friedrich Nietzsche tarnished his reputation for a generation, as we shall soon see. This is unfortunate, given how little the Soviet system had to do in practice with the ideas of Karl Marx. In 1917 Russia was still a feudal society that attempted to jump directly into communism without ever having passed through capitalism, thus violating Marx's theory of historical development through a sequence of stages. The gradual evolution of capitalism into a post-industrial form in the West, rather than its apocalyptic collapse, has refuted Marx's analysis, as have the rise of the welfare state and the expansion of the middle class, neither of which he predicted. Ironically, the development of fiscal and monetary stabilizing policies in the twentieth century, designed to limit the destructiveness of the business cycle of boom and bust, was partly inspired by Marx; as a result, his thought has been described as a 'self-defeating prophecy' that helped to save capitalism.

Nevertheless, the financial crisis that began in the West in 2008 has stimulated much interest in Marx's portrait of capitalism as a system prone to increasing inequality, instability and unfairness. Political scientists are now describing the American political system as more plutocratic, rule by the wealthy, than democratic, and some economists have recently argued that capitalism in the long run does create wealth faster for the rich than for the rest. Meanwhile, conditions in developing capitalist economies in our time, such as China and India, remain very similar to those of the nineteenth-century West that Marx analysed and reviled. This shows that, as long as capitalism exists, in whatever form, Marx's work will almost certainly be needed to diagnose its illnesses and ultimately, perhaps, one day to stand as its obituary.

22

Friedrich Nietzsche: The Psychologist

The curse of mental illness stalked Friedrich Nietzsche for his entire life. His father died of 'softening of the brain' when his son was just five. The crippling headaches, loss of vision, violent mood swings, depression and vomiting that were the main symptoms of his own mental problems first struck him when he was a teenager and continued, with increasing severity, for the next three decades. Finally he collapsed into complete madness, from which he never recovered. Thereafter, he lived on for another decade as a total invalid until his death in 1900. The affliction that cost him his sanity had earlier cost him his career as a professor at the University of Basel, from which he retired on a modest pension at the age of just 35. He then led the life of a lonely wanderer in the years that followed, writing the works for which he is now so famous, none of which was successful in his own lifetime. The nature of Nietzsche's illness has never been conclusively diagnosed.

Nietzsche insisted that pain and illness are blessings, since they stimulate the imagination and give the afflicted a depth that is lacking among the healthy. 'Great pain is the ultimate liberator of the spirit', he declared. He believed that his most intellectually productive moments coincided with his worst suffering. He also used the language of disease in his 'diagnosis' of modern civilization. He wanted to replace the language of good and evil, virtue and vice, with the language of sickness and health, weakness and strength. It is a 'madman' that is Nietzsche's prophet of a new age who announces the 'death of God' to the uncomprehending masses in his book *The Gay Science*. The nihilism that he believed must follow in the wake of the West's loss of faith in the Christian God was something that he thought could and should be overcome. The antidote that he prescribed for this condition was the 'supermen', exceptional geniuses whose overflowing creativity and will-to-power only flourish when released from the straitjacket of morality, which he saw as a kind of sickness. Now that belief in all gods is dead, Nietzsche claimed that Western civilization finds itself on an open sea unbounded by traditional moral constraints, where great and terrible things are again possible. If he had not struggled with mental illness, he might never have come to this important insight, or so he was convinced.

It is perhaps because Nietzsche struggled with his own inner demons that he often described himself as a psychologist with a special talent in 'the art of psychological analysis', as he called it. Both Sigmund Freud and Carl Jung agreed, so much so that the great Viennese psychoanalyst deliberately avoided any systematic study of Nietzsche's works; he knew just enough about them to sense that many of his own theories had already been anticipated by Nietzsche, something that threatened his claims to originality. Nietzsche was also drawn to psychology as a substitute for traditional philosophy, with which he had grown bitterly disillusioned. He preferred to 'refute' ideas by psychologizing them. In his hands psychology was a method (or weapon) for exposing the often perverse and unseemly motives (as he saw them) behind the lofty ideas of thinkers he disagreed with, such as Plato, Rousseau and Kant. Nietzsche treated their views as symptoms of underlying mental pathologies. 'A thinker cannot do other than convert his physical condition into the most highly intellectual of forms', he wrote. 'This act of transformation *is* philosophy'. However unfair this method might be, his writings abound with penetrating psychological insights and brilliant, often witty, analyses of people and their psychological relationship to their own ideas, as Nietzsche saw them, a technique that works very effectively in his own case too, as he was the first to admit.

'Fritz', as Nietzsche was known to his family, was the son of a Lutheran pastor who was descended from several generations of Protestant clergymen. His mother was the daughter of a minister as well, and Nietzsche was born close to the birthplace of Martin Luther, whose legacy still dominated the religious culture of the region. (Nietzsche and Luther were born 70 kilometres apart, in what is now Saxony-Anhalt.) This background did not prevent Nietzsche from coming to see Christianity as the source and symbol of everything he most despised; indeed, it probably played a decisive part in his eventual rejection of Christianity, against which he waged a personal campaign in the pages of his books, one of which is titled *The Anti-Christ*. He rebelled against the whole social, political, moral and religious order of Europe in which his parents raised him. It was Christianity, he believed, that had spread a slave revolt in morals initiated by the downcast ancient

Jews, who were motivated by resentment and envy against their powerful oppressors. Unable to defeat them by force, Nietzsche argued, Jews and later Christians won a non-violent moral victory over their masters by inventing the concepts of 'good' and 'evil' to legitimize the values and interests of slaves. That is the 'genealogy' of the moral system that has dominated the West ever since, which Nietzsche believed was inimical to all greatness. He viewed Christian anti-Semitism as just a ruse designed to hide the deep alliance of these co-conspirators against the strong and healthy. He also described Christianity as a Jewish conspiracy to conquer the world on behalf of the sick and the weak, who should naturally be controlled by the healthy and the strong.

For Nietzsche, morality is a human invention with a beginning and an end, and we have now reached that end in the Christian West. Just as the pre-Christian, aristocratic warrior societies of antiquity existed *before* good and evil, Nietzsche prophesied that the post-Christian world of the future would exist *beyond* good and evil (the title of another of his books). He was convinced that the Christian God had become unbelievable in the modern West, and everything that rested on that faith, 'the whole of our European morality', must collapse with it. In the void left by the loss of belief in Christianity and its moral system Nietzsche saw a unique opportunity to establish new, aristocratic, non-moral values suitable for masters rather than slaves.

Nietzsche was sketchy about what, precisely, he had in mind for this new, post-Christian world, partly because it would be the future creation of the 'higher form of species' that would dominate it, the so-called 'supermen'. The point is that such 'free spirits' would conform to no existing or established rules or restrictions that might interfere with their overflowing creativity and natural dominance. Impelled by a restless 'will-to-power', these Olympian individuals would create great things on a blank and boundless canvas, pitilessly using 'lesser' people as 'clay' with which to mould new works. For Nietzsche, man is just an 'ugly stone' that needs a sculptor in the form of the superman. That is why he wrote approvingly of 'the sacrifice of countless people who have to be pushed down and shrunk into incomplete human beings, into slaves, into tools, all for the sake of the aristocracy'. All of this first requires smashing the shackles of Christian morality and repudiating the 'slave' values of pity, sympathy and compassion that it represents. The ancient Greeks that Nietzsche admired were subject to no such decadent sentiments, which is why they were able to reach the summit of human artistic achievement and why modern civilization languishes in the creative depths.

Past 'sculptors' whose consciences never troubled them when sacrificing the lives and wellbeing of large numbers of ordinary men and women in order to impose their will on the world include Alexander the Great, Julius Caesar, Cesare Borgia and Napoleon. Nietzsche admired all of these ruthless, strong-willed 'artist-tyrants'. But the modern man whom he most revered and who was his exemplar of greatness was a pure artist, rather than an artist-tyrant: the modern German poet and writer Goethe.

The main goal and purpose of the supermen is to create culture and values to fill the void left by Christian morality, and politics would be subordinated to that goal. But, in a world beyond good and evil, anything is possible, so the occasional artist-tyrant such as Napoleon is bound to arise to impose his preferred form ruthlessly on human affairs according to his overflowing will-to-power. That is why Nietzsche admired Napoleon as an 'artist of government'.

Given all this, it is difficult to speak of a Nietzschean politics. He prescribed no positive political system or goals, let alone a theory. He saw himself as the prophet of a coming post-Christian, post-moral world that would be wholly dominated by artists who would be free to shape it according to their own super-abundant will-to-power. For Nietzsche, art is 'the supreme task and the truly metaphysical activity in this life'. Nietzschean politics serves artistic ends. The greatest art (including the art of politics) is achieved by the ideal balancing of what Nietzsche called the 'Dionysian' principle of unbounded, intoxicating passion and pure will (named after Dionysus, the son of Zeus and the Greek god of wine and dance) and the 'Apollonian' principle of order, harmony and good form (named after Apollo, another son of Zeus and the Greek god of the sun). The result is 'passion controlled' in the form of great works of beauty and power that balance opposites in an original and aesthetically pleasing way.

According to Nietzsche, the superman must first subdue himself before imposing his will on the external world. He must be a warrior on the internal battlefield of the soul and engage in a process of 'self-overcoming', shaping himself (psychologically) before he is in a position to shape the external world. Nietzsche favoured the controlled and self-disciplined expression of natural impulses in order to create beauty and establish values, which are never the result of blind, uncontrolled urges. Much as he admired the healthy, brutish, conscience-free urge to dominate in Vikings and samurai warriors, particularly compared to the life-denying sheepishness and mediocrity of Christians and democrats, his ultimate ideal was of a higher order. The natural will-to-power must be expressed through and disciplined by the creative imagination, as it was, *par excellence*, in the tragic plays of ancient Greece. This means organizing one's own inner chaos of emotions and drives by creating a unified self in which one drive dominates all of the others and, thereby, defines you and becomes your personal 'style'. The creation of the self is therefore the necessary first creation of the artist.

It is not difficult to see why Nietzsche's views proved popular with the Nazis and why he came to be regarded by many as a fascist philosopher. His writings are full of references to 'blond beasts' and the 'will-to-power', and he saw himself as the prophet of a brutal, amoral warrior ethic for a new race of naturally superior 'supermen' who will reduce the inferior masses of ordinary people to slavery. The irony of this association is that Nietzsche was a passionate opponent of German nationalism (he called the Germans a 'servile race') and often criticized anti-Semitism. He was openly disdainful of his sister Elizabeth's anti-Semitic views and chose to live and work outside Germany for most of his adult life. Nietzsche was also an elitist and an individualist with an instinctive contempt for the 'herd' and a profound distaste for the kind of populist demagoguery that Hitler and the Nazis represented. It is very likely that, had he lived long enough, he would have found the Nazis to epitomize what he most despised about mass society and mainstream politics.

Unfortunately for Nietzsche's posthumous reputation, Adolf Hitler paid a much-publicized visit to the Nietzsche Archive in Weimar at the invitation of its founder and director, the philosopher's sister Elizabeth, who was an ardent Nazi. Hitler had come with his personal photographer Heinrich Hoffmann, who took a picture of the Führer contemplating a large bust of Nietzsche in the archive's main reception room. The photograph was widely published in the German press and featured in Hoffmann's popular biography, *Hitler as Nobody Knows Him*, with the following caption: 'The Führer before the bust of the German philosopher whose ideas have fertilized two great popular movements: the National Socialist of Germany and the Fascist of Italy'. Hoffmann's unfortunate photograph cemented the popular association between Nietzsche and the Nazis for several generations, and all but destroyed Nietzsche's credibility in post-war Europe for decades to come.

Nietzsche's reputation has not only recovered from this unfair association with Nazism but is now higher than ever before. He is now among the most widely read and quoted writers in the history of ideas, to a degree that would surely have surprised and even appalled a thinker who was openly contemptuous of popular opinion. 'Books for everybody are always malodorous books', he wrote, with a strong hint of sour grapes when his own books did not sell well. 'The smell of petty people clings to them.' It is Nietzsche's diagnosis of the crisis of Western civilization that continues to resonate in our time rather than his proposal for curing it, which was much worse than the illness. Fortunately, only a small, if noisy, fringe now take Nietzsche's prescription seriously. But his analysis of and attacks on the basic assumptions that underlie modern liberal democratic societies today are not so easily dismissed as the products of a diseased mind. For example, many secular liberals have long argued

that modern liberalism, egalitarianism and human rights
stem from the rejection of Christianity during the French
Enlightenment. But Nietzsche insisted that these modern
principles were actually the direct products of Christian
morality, with its concern for the poorest and weakest
human beings. Historians of Western moral sentiments are
now coming to agree with Nietzsche's genealogy, if not with
his dim assessment of it. This has not only challenged the
self-image of the modern age but has tied the fate of many
of its core values to the loss of religious belief, raising the
spectre of moral nihilism that Nietzsche warned was the
central crisis of modernity.

Contemporaries

23

Mohandas Gandhi: The Warrior

Too often Gandhi is portrayed as a gentle and saintly holy man. He was, above all, a fighter for justice – all too ready, perhaps, to sacrifice his own life and the lives of his followers. What Gandhi admired most was fearlessness, and he unflinchingly faced deadly attacks throughout his life. In the campaign he waged against Defence Minister Jan Smuts on behalf of Indians working in South Africa, Gandhi perfected his strategy of non-violent boycotts, marches and strikes – pressuring the government to rescind its racist laws. During these battles, Gandhi endured nearly 20 years of beatings, attempted lynchings and appalling prison conditions. In January 1914 the European railway workers in South Africa went on a general strike for economic reasons, threatening the survival of the white minority government. Immediately, Gandhi called off his own previously announced protest march on the grounds that it would be wrong to take advantage of his adversary's weakness. Gandhi's surprise concession caught Smuts off guard. One of Smuts's secretaries described his quandary to Gandhi:

I do not like your people, and do not care to assist them at all. But what am I to do? You help us in our days of need. How can we lay hands on you? I often wish you took to violence like the English strikers, and then we would know at once how to dispose of you. But you will not injure even the enemy. You desire victory by self-suffering alone and will never transgress your self-imposed limits of courtesy and chivalry. And that is what reduces us to sheer helplessness.

By June 1914, Gandhi and Smuts had negotiated a new Indian Relief Bill, restoring basic rights to the South African Indian community. The next month, Gandhi set sail for India with the mission of freeing his homeland from centuries of unjust British rule while preserving friendship between India and Britain. Gandhi's Indian campaign was ultimately successful but at a horrific cost to himself and others – a cost culminating in Gandhi's own assassination by a fellow Hindu in 1948. His enemies, whether in South Africa or India, confronted his highly unorthodox tactics in five stages: indifference, ridicule, abuse, repression and finally, respect. Indeed, Jan Smuts became a lifelong friend and admirer of his once despised Indian opponent.

Gandhi was a brilliant strategist of human conflict, the Napoleon of non-violence. What makes him unique among the great warriors in history is that he achieved victories against much more powerful opponents by combining a courageous willingness to suffer and even to die with an equally resolute determination not to injure or kill. Gandhi believed that violence was the weapon of the weak, who kill out of a fear of dying. Gandhi hated above all the timorous submission to oppression: better to die on your feet than to live on your knees. He was not surprised that the most warlike of the Indians (the Pathans) were also the greatest practitioners of non-violent resistance. You cannot teach non-violence, he often said, to a coward. Gandhi himself was decorated by the British government for his courageous service in combat as an ambulance driver during the Boer War (1899–1902).

Gandhi was the product of the highest ideals of the Christian West and the Indian East. Born in India, he travelled to London as a young man to become a lawyer. He developed a great respect for British law and liberties; his whole life could be described as an attempt to get the British rulers of South Africa and India to live up to their own ideals of legal justice. While in London, this future Indian monk wore a top hat and tails, learned ballroom dancing, studied Latin and French and took up the violin. More importantly, Gandhi met in London a motley crew of devout Christian and ex-Christian pacifists, vegetarians, feminists and socialists. Ironically, Gandhi's exploration of Christian ideals in London ultimately led him back to his Hindu roots. The first of his experimental communes (later known as Ashrams) was named Tolstoy Farm, after the great Russian novelist and Christian pacifist. Gandhi was the least sectarian of religious sages in history: his fellow Hindus sometimes complained that he seemed too Christian. He insisted upon equal respect for all of the world's major religions. Whatever religion you inherit, he would say, you should try to become the best exemplar of that religion.

The seeds of Gandhi's ideal of non-violent resistance are found in his encounter with the Jesus of the Gospels. Gandhi always referred to Jesus as the greatest practitioner of non-violent resistance. Jesus says to the Jews living under Roman oppression: 'If anyone strikes you on the right cheek, turn the other also; and if anyone wants to sue you and take your coat, give your cloak as well; and if anyone forces you to go one mile, go also the second mile'. By Roman law a soldier was permitted to require a civilian to carry his pack for one mile. So, Jesus says, when a Roman soldier unjustly demands that you carry his pack for one mile, offer to carry it two miles. Why answer Roman evil with goodness? By punishing yourself, you throw the crime of the oppressor back into his face. If your oppressor has any conscience, he will feel the sting of your rebuke. Gandhi's Jesus is a champion of active non-violent resistance against the Roman empire, not a meek advocate of passive non-resistance to evil.

Gandhi's quest for holiness was both personal and political. Even as a young man, he became increasingly troubled by his own sexual and other appetites. He yearned for inner serenity and a philosophical detachment from his own bodily urges. At the same time, as a young lawyer working in South Africa, he also became increasingly disturbed by the lust for domination among the whites and the craven submission of the non-white races he witnessed. As soon as he arrived in South Africa, Gandhi himself was ejected from a first-class train carriage simply because of his colour. His vocation was to see a relationship between personal psychology and social oppression. Like the American naturalist and radical Henry David Thoreau, like John Ruskin and like Leo Tolstoy, Gandhi became convinced that modern capitalism, by fanning the flames of desire for more and more commodities, by stimulating envy and social competition, was creating the psychological

basis for class and race oppression. Following the example
of his hero, Socrates, Gandhi always insisted that peace and
justice in the world depended upon peace and harmony
within each human soul. Hence, his campaigns for social
justice were always rooted in the self-discipline of his
ascetic communes, devoted to voluntary poverty.

Gandhi's asceticism was a worldly one, in service to peace
and justice. All soldiers must be rigorously disciplined so
that they can ignore their bodily appetites and learn to
accept suffering and even death. The same applies to monks,
whose ascetic practices are precisely such a training: by
learning to sacrifice smaller desires and appetites, they
ultimately become capable of sacrificing their own lives.
The courage required for non-violent resistance rests upon
years of ascetic training in self-control, self-purification and
suffering. Gandhi's followers took formal vows of chastity,
poverty and service; they were required to fast, exercise,
work and pray. These practices of self-perfection were both
an end in themselves and a means to cultivate courageous
warriors for social justice. Individual self-perfection lays
the necessary foundation for healing the world. Gandhi
famously insisted that a person must first become the
change he seeks to see in the world.

Gandhi coined a new word to describe his worldly
asceticism, *satyagraha*, based on the Hindu word *satya*,
meaning 'reality' or 'truth'. *Satyagraha* means 'firmness
in pursuit of the truth'; Gandhi once explained it as 'the
conquest of one's adversary by suffering in one's own
person'. The fruit of *satyagraha* is the courage of non-violent
resistance, or *ahimsa*. If we are willing to die, then there is
no need for violence to protect our lives. Ascetic discipline
is traditionally reserved for elite spiritual athletes. No

religious tradition has expected it of everyone. But Gandhi was convinced that virtually anyone was capable of this rigorous discipline: he aimed to democratize the ascetic ideal. His strict vegan diet nearly killed his wife, his children and himself, and his relations with his family were strained, to put it mildly, by other disciplines. Gandhi-ism was not possible even for all the Gandhis. As for his mass followers, many resorted to shocking violence during his various campaigns, especially in India. He spent the final 30 years of his life working for Hindu–Muslim friendship in a unified India, only to see at the end widespread pogroms, brutal inter-communal violence and the first Indo-Pakistani war. Although India and Pakistan did achieve independence without ever fighting Britain, Gandhi considered his life's work a total failure.

Gandhi was both a warrior and a sage. He was the most philosophical of politicians and the most political of philosophers. In addition to his theories of truth, violence and asceticism, Gandhi rethought the whole relation between ends and means in politics. He always insisted that violence and non-violence were not two means to the same end – say, Indian independence. He well understood that the resort to violence creates a very different future from the use of non-violence. First, each of us shapes our own character by what we choose to do or to suffer. If we choose violence, then we will become violent. How can true peace be created by violent people? Second, as a chivalric warrior, Gandhi always looked forward to reconciliation and friendship with his opponents. By fighting with the sword of love and the armour of truth, he created the basis for harmony with his former enemies. Third, Gandhi well appreciated the uncertainties of politics: we can be sure only of our present choices. So sacrificing the good that can be done today for an uncertain future made no sense to him. Our means become our ends: only peaceful means can lead to true peace. For Gandhi, non-violence was not only a policy but also an ethical creed.

Gandhi argued that his creed of non-violent resistance was both universally applicable and morally pure. The logic of non-violent resistance is to punish oneself for the crime of one's oppressor, so as to rebuke his conscience. If one's oppressor has no conscience, then the non-violent appeal to that conscience will fail. Nation-states do not generally have a conscience, so pacifism between states usually means appeasement of aggressors: even Gandhi denounced the appeasement of Hitler in the Munich Agreement of 1938. In Nazi and communist regimes, vicious ideologies have wholly or partly occluded the humane conscience of the agents of those regimes. Non-violent resistance cannot check evil where no appeal to a humane conscience is possible. General Smuts might be moved, but not Heinrich Himmler. Moreover, Gandhian politics depends upon free communication for the co-ordination of direct action. If all the leaders of non-violent resistance were suddenly to disappear, what hope would there be for any collective action? For these reasons, Gandhian politics only works in countries enjoying basic civil liberties. When asked about the Jews in Nazi Germany, all Gandhi could suggest was mass suicide.

If not universally applicable, is Gandhian non-violence morally pure? Unfortunately, collective action always victimizes innocent third parties. Gandhi's boycotts against the government in India caused the sacking of sympathetic textile workers in Lancashire. Boycotts and strikes always impose harms and costs upon many people who are not party to the conflict. Moreover, Gandhi's own self-punishing fasts appeared to many of his contemporaries as a form of moral blackmail. In those 'fasts unto death', he threatened his opponents: 'unless you stop what you are doing, I'll starve myself'. This may not be as coercive as killing, but it is still coercive. Politics is impossible without coercion of some kind. Gandhi's non-violent coercion is often both more effective and morally superior to violent coercion, but even a non-violent politics cannot be morally pure.

Gandhi's genius was to show, however, that ascetic discipline can help to sustain a heroic politics of non-violent resistance. His most famous successor was the Revd Dr Martin Luther King, who trained his followers in the techniques of non-violent protest and patient suffering. King's non-violent politics aimed to remove the laws enforcing racial segregation in the American south: he succeeded because of the existence of basic civil liberties in the United States, and because the conscience of most American southerners was not deaf to the appeal of racial justice. Perhaps the most dramatic successes of Gandhian politics were achieved in Eastern Europe in 1989. Massive protest crowds patiently endured actual and threatened violence for months, bringing down communist regimes in Poland, Czechoslovakia, Romania, Bulgaria, Hungary, East Germany and the Baltic states. If a large enough mass of people decides not to co-operate with evil, no regime can survive. Political scientists are discovering that non-violent protests are usually the most effective means of removing oppressive regimes.

Gandhian politics does not work everywhere, and it is not morally pure. But, in most cases, it offers a better path to social and political justice than violence does. In his day, Gandhi's politics was often denounced by progressives as medieval and reactionary. Yet the future seems likely to belong to this monk and warrior for peace.

24

Sayyid Qutb: The Jihadist

In 1948, an idealistic teacher of modern literature seeking professional training travelled from his home in Cairo, Egypt, to the small, conservative, dry, rural town of Greeley, Colorado, in the American West, to study at the Colorado State Teachers College. This teacher, Sayyid Qutb, certainly received an education in Greeley – and at other American campuses he visited – but not one he was expecting. He wrote letters home from the US expressing his horror at what he considered the shameless sexual promiscuity, the obsession with brutal sports and the worship of the almighty dollar. Like most travellers, Qutb learned more about his own country and beliefs than about the country he was visiting: the shock of American co-education ('the animal-like mixing of the sexes'), American materialism and racism turned Qutb from a moderate to a radical Islamist. Greeley, Colorado, thus may be viewed as the improbable birthplace of modern militant Islam.

Soon after returning from the US, Qutb joined the Society of Muslim Brothers in Egypt. He supported Gamal Nasser's military coup but soon fell out with the more secular general. Gaoled by Nasser, Qutb was repeatedly tortured but still managed to write a six-volume commentary on the Qur'an while in prison before he was hanged in 1966 – making him the first great martyr of modern political Islam. Many Westerners often assume that militant Islam is primarily directed against Christians or Jews, but Qutb's life, thought and death show that modern Islamic radicalism is directed primarily against the governments of Muslim countries – and Westerners who support those governments. It is impossible to begin to understand religiously motivated violence without first understanding that Christians have mainly killed other Christians, Jews other Jews and Muslims other Muslims. Religious violence is primarily fraternal, as we saw with the assassination of Gandhi by a fellow Hindu.

Like many devout Christians, Jews and Muslims, Qutb was deeply disturbed by the secularism of modern life, in which religion had retreated to occasional services on the Sabbath. In his view, modern people act like mere animals during the working week by eating, sleeping, shopping, earning and procreating with no thought of God, becoming spiritual beings only during Sabbath worship. Qutb rejected this division of human beings into everyday materialists who become spiritual only at the mosque. True happiness is possible only by integrating the whole of life into devotion to God, so that every meal, every job, every friendship, every act of parenting becomes a kind of prayer to the Holy One. Qutb's ideal of a truly Islamic society is not an ascetic world of constant self-denial but an integrated world in which all the pleasures of life are fully enjoyed within the moderate and humane bounds of Islamic law. Islam, he says, demands our whole lives, not merely Sabbath worship. We shall never be happy until our material and our spiritual pursuits are fully integrated. Islam, he says, is not a religion; it is a whole way of life.

Militant Islam is often accused of being medieval and reactionary. Qutb routinely appealed to a vision of the first generation of Muslims as the standard by which to judge the subsequent corruption of Islam. But Qutbian Islam, like other fundamentalisms, is thoroughly modern. In traditional Islam, the Qur'an is studied in the light of various traditions of interpretation and schools of jurisprudence. Qutb rejects all of these, calling for a return to the pure Qur'anic text – as interpreted by himself. In traditional Muslim societies, there are many intermediaries between Islamic law and individual Muslims, including ethnic customs, tribal elders, jurists and kings. Qutb wants to sweep all of them away so that each individual Muslim can be ruled by Islamic law alone. In place of traditional social and religious hierarchies, he offers radical equality; in place of traditional political authorities, he offers radical freedom from human domination. According to Qutb, the modern ideals of liberty, equality and fraternity are possible only through the submission of every individual person to God alone.

Qutb's vision of divine sovereignty cannot be understood apart from the biblical and Qur'anic portrait of a jealous God, who insists that we are loyal to Him alone: 'You shall have no gods besides me'. The Abrahamic religions are committed not merely to divine monotheism but also to divine monogamy: God does not tolerate infidelity – that is, worshipping other gods. Qutb insists that when human beings put their trust in wealth, military power, technology or human governments, we are guilty of that same infidelity. Divine sovereignty means that we must not submit to any human power but only to God. Qutb is certainly right that modern theories of political sovereignty are incompatible with divine sovereignty. If a human government is sovereign, then God cannot be sovereign; if God is sovereign, then no government can be sovereign. Sovereignty by definition is indivisible. All modern governments claim to be sovereign, thus denying God's sovereignty. Qutb rejects the idea that God somehow appoints earthly rulers and shares his sovereignty with them: God is a jealous God who demands complete loyalty. 'No god but God' means no sovereignty but God's, no law but God's and no authority but God's.

Because there is only one God, there is also only one people. Traditionally, Islam has had a special relationship to Arabia, to the Arabic language and to the larger Arab nation. Qutb insists, however, that all of these national and cultural distinctions must be swept away into a global community of Islam. He attacks Judaism for being merely a tribal religion and Christianity for being a merely spiritual one. Islam alone, he says, is universal and holistic, providing a guide to personal, familial, economic, social and political life for every human being.

The word 'Islam' means 'submission', and Qutb argues that true freedom is possible only by total submission to God. When we obey human beings, he says, we sink into servitude because we become subject to an arbitrary human will. Obedience to God means submission to a perfectly rational and just will. This kind of submission creates true human freedom. According to Rousseau, submission to any particular human will is servitude while submission to 'the general will' is freedom. Qutb agrees with Rousseau, although he argues that the only truly general will is the divine will, not the popular will.

Qutb's ideal Islamic ruler, a caliph or imam, has no independent authority and no power to legislate. He is merely God's deputy – responsible for interpreting, applying and enforcing Islamic law. Qutb's ideal regime is the rule of God (literally, a theocracy). But since theocracy has come to mean the rule of priests, Qutb denies that Islam could be a theocracy since it has no priests. The Islamic ruler lacks the sacred authority of priests or holy men; the caliph is merely a first among equals. Each caliph should be chosen by the Muslim people. So long as the caliph enforces Islamic law and only Islamic law, the people are obliged to obey him.

Qutb is most notorious for his theory of jihad. He has been called 'the philosopher of Islamic terror' – even though he insists that women and children may never be attacked. Jihad for Qutb begins with a spiritual fight against temptation. He argues that no one can fight effectively for social justice who has not conquered injustice within himself. Although preaching, testifying and witnessing to one's faith are kinds of jihad, Qutb is clear that jihad also means 'kill and be killed'. He defends jihad as a kind of holy war against those who are ignorant of God, pointing out that it is endorsed by the Old Testament and was practised by Christians during the Crusades. Traditionally, jihad was justified first to eliminate paganism from Arabia and then to defend the Muslim homelands from invading non-believers. Qutb's innovation is to transform this defensive (and tribal) jihad into a global struggle to establish Islam. He pioneers a jihad directed primarily against the Muslim rulers of Islamic societies.

Qutbian jihad is a natural consequence of his religious holism. If Islam means a complete way of life, then Muslims must fight for control over every aspect of personal, social, religious and political activity. Islam cannot be a private religious belief or practice segregated from the rest of economic and political life. 'Freedom of religion' for Muslims, he says, is meaningless unless Muslims can live out their religion in every aspect of life. Significantly, this means that Muslims can tolerate Christian and Jewish minorities within an Islamic polity, but Muslims cannot live their faith as a minority within a non-Muslim polity.

How is jihad compatible with religious liberty for all? According to Qutb, the Qur'an endorses both principles: 'fight them until there is no more oppression and all submission is to God alone' and 'there shall be no compulsion in religion'. So long as Muslims live in a society that does not conform in every aspect to Islam, they are religiously oppressed, even by Muslim rulers. But a truly Islamic polity tolerates the religious liberty of Jewish and Christian minorities, who can fully practise their religions. Once an Islamic polity is established, then jihad takes the form of preaching and witnessing to the faith, which will one day win over most Jews and Christians. Hence, jihad creates the conditions for universal and true religious liberty.

Many Westerners argue that Islam needs to experience a reformation in order to become compatible with modern liberalism. But militant Islam already is a would-be Reformation. Like the early Lutherans and Calvinists of the Protestant Reformation, Qutb denounces the corruption of the clergy, the theologians and the jurists. Luther's slogan was 'Scripture alone' while Qutb's is 'Qur'an alone'. Just as the Calvinists sought to restore the pristine purity of 'primitive' Christianity, so Qutb advocates a return to the pure Islam of the first generation of Muslims. Over the centuries Islam, like Catholic Christianity, had acquired many religious customs not found in Scripture, such as forms of mysticism, liturgies, veneration of martyrs and shrines, processions and religious music and art. Militant Islam is just as iconoclastic as Calvinism: all of these traditional religious customs and forms of art are violently attacked as mere idolatry. The Puritans created political communities governed by biblical law alone, just as Qutb seeks a world ruled by Qur'anic law alone.

Qutb believed that human beings are religious animals more than economic animals. If Marx claimed that 'religion is the opiate of the masses', then Qutb claims that both Marxism and capitalism are the true opiates of the masses. Modern politicians 'drug' people with ever greater material resources when what people really want is more spiritual meaning. Many people today are surprised that twentieth-century secular revolutions in Algeria, Libya, Egypt, Israel, India and Pakistan have provoked religious counter-revolutions in all those nations. Qutb would not be. If human nature yearns for knowledge of the one God, then no amount of economic or technological progress will answer those yearnings. In retrospect, it is the secular progressivists of the mid-twentieth century who appear naïve about human nature. According to Qutb, all political conflict is theological conflict at the root. Western imperialism is not about economic or political power but about Christian hegemony. Our only choice in politics is whether to honour the true God or some false idol of our own making.

As Westerners discovered during the Protestant Reformation, nothing is so revolutionary as a return to the past. Qutb's return to the Qur'an promises an equally dramatic transformation of our world. Earlier in this book, we noted that the first Islamic political philosopher, Al-Farabi, was confident that Islam could incorporate the best of Western philosophy and science. Qutb, by contrast, is fearful that Islam will become fatally contaminated by the very same Western arts and sciences. The fate of the world now largely depends on which of these two contrasting forms of Islam prevails.

25

Hannah Arendt: The Pariah

Hannah Arendt narrowly escaped from the Nazis twice. In 1933 she was arrested by the Gestapo in Berlin and held for eight days. After her release she promptly fled to Paris, where, as a Jew, she was later stripped of her German citizenship. (She would remain a stateless person until she became a US citizen after the war.) The Nazis caught up with her again when they invaded France in 1940. She was interned as an 'enemy alien' in a camp near the Spanish border. Luckily, in the chaos caused by the fall of France that summer, Arendt was allowed to leave the camp. She lay low until the new puppet government installed by the Nazis briefly relaxed its exit permit policy, when Arendt and her husband made their escape to America. When she arrived in the US in 1941 (she was 35), she had just $25 in her pocket and only a limited knowledge of English. All of the works for which she became well known had yet to be written. But her background as a persecuted victim of a totalitarian regime forced into exile (twice) had by then indelibly shaped her outlook on politics. So it was that Arendt began to write the book that would first bring her to public notice, *The Origins of Totalitarianism*.

Arendt's greatest public notoriety came in the early 1960s, with the publication of her book *Eichmann in Jerusalem*, which first appeared in *The New Yorker* magazine. She was the magazine's reporter in 1961 at Adolf Eichmann's war crimes trial in Israel for his role in the Nazi Holocaust. Arendt's surprising portrait of him as a banal and thoughtless bureaucrat of genocide, someone 'terrifyingly normal' rather than a raving, fanatical Nazi ideologue, was highly controversial at the time (and is today hotly disputed), as were the questions she raised about the legality of the trial itself. She also provocatively accused some Zionists of holding outdated nationalist views that grew out of the same nineteenth-century *völkisch* soil as German nationalism. Worst of all, her harsh judgement of Jews who worked for the Nazi-authorized Jewish Councils during the war led to bitter accusations that she was 'victim blaming' by implying their complicity in the Holocaust. Having been a pariah among her fellow Germans before the war as a Jew, she found herself a pariah among many of her fellow Jews after it as well. And if not exactly a pariah in the United States, Arendt, an émigrée European intellectual and independent woman, remained a stranger to the mass consumer society of post-war middle America, where she spent the rest of her life.

As a young woman in pre-war Germany, Arendt had studied philosophy and theology rather than politics, which was then of little interest to her. All of that changed when the Nazis came to power in 1933 and she was forced to flee for her life. Twenty years later, in the United States, her outlook had changed completely. Now Arendt viewed politics as having an independent value and vital importance little understood or appreciated in the modern world. She criticized the domination of politics by philosophy, a tendency she traced all the way back to Plato. Almost without exception since then, Arendt alleged, philosophers have shared this original anti-political bias at the origins of Western thought, which has deformed public life and impaired our capacity for judgement, often with disastrous consequences. Against this long tradition of thinking Arendt hoped to recover the original Greek understanding of politics, according to which participation in public life is essential to our humanity and not just a necessary evil, as Thomas Paine had described it. For her, Western philosophers since Plato have missed the vital existential importance of political action and denied its inherent dignity. This led some of her critics to accuse her of Hellenic nostalgia and an anti-intellectual hostility to philosophy.

The clearest expression of this outlook appears in Arendt's most important political book, *The Human Condition*, which is an account of the original Greek meaning of politics and why man is, essentially, a political animal, as Aristotle had claimed. The work distinguishes between three categories of activity: labour, work and action.

Arendt argues that, for the ancient Greeks, labour is the lowest and most basic human activity, which we share with all animals. It is the closest to nature and aims to sustain life itself by satisfying our fundamental biological needs, such as eating. In contrast, work goes beyond mere physical survival by engaging in activities that produce a world of enduring objects such as technology, architecture and painting that are not merely consumed to keep us alive. This is something that animals never do. That is why the ancient Greeks rated work above labour, according to

Arendt. Highest of all for them, by far, is action, the realm of politics, which they saw as the shared public space where free citizens meet and debate the common affairs of their city and, in doing so, exercise their powers of agency, disclose their individual identities and affirm a common public world. Nothing was more human for them, Arendt tells us, than this particular form of coming together, which she saw as the essence of politics in ancient Greece. The lesser activities of labour and work were strictly confined to the private sphere (the household, the farm, the workshop, the market-place), which is governed by necessity, whereas action occurs only in the public sphere, which is the realm of freedom. For Arendt, freedom is experienced only by active citizens participating in public affairs, not by private individuals left alone to do as they please, free from politics.

In the classical world of the Greek city-states, as Arendt presents it, the political arena was where citizens transcended nature and human identity was formed through collective action. We need to act and speak together in a common public space in order to affirm our own shared reality. That is why the Greeks referred contemptuously to a citizen who concerned himself exclusively with his own private affairs as an *idiótēs*, an idiot, in contrast to a *polítēs*, a citizen devoted above all to the public good. Philosophers who chose to neglect public duties to pursue philosophy and slaves who were excluded from politics as non-citizens were both idiots in the original Greek sense of the word because, in Arendt's words, 'to live an entirely private life means above all to be deprived of things essential to a truly human life'. This is an affirmation of Aristotle's central claim that we cannot live a truly human life outside of politics, although she believed that politics is a human creation as far from nature as it is possible for us to get, whereas Aristotle asserted that we are political animals by nature. Hobbes and Locke were wrong to defend politics primarily as a means of preserving life: it exists primarily to give human life meaning, according to Arendt.

According to Arendt, there is a natural political affinity between philosophers and tyranny. Philosophers claim knowledge of the truth and are tempted to impose it on the rest of us, by force if necessary. That is why Plato opposed democracy in favour of rule by benevolent philosopher-kings. He saw governing as a science that an enlightened elite, with the right training, can learn and practise in the interests of everyone. Such paternalistic rule is really the opposite of the original Greek understanding of politics, as Arendt sees it, as a public sharing of words and deeds among a plurality of citizens who thereby create a common world rather than seek the truth. For Arendt, abandoning politics to an elite of philosopher-kings, ideologues, technocrats or enlightened despots is ruinous for humanity, which requires this shared public world to hold citizens together artificially. The historical tragedy of the Jews, she argued, is that they have been political pariahs who were shut out of the public sphere, which has deprived them of their humanity and sense of political reality. This was something she feared was becoming a general feature of the modern age, leaving it vulnerable to a range of political pathologies such as totalitarianism and tribal nationalism. The best defence against these malevolent tendencies is a recovery of the original Greek conception of politics and, as she sees it, a restoration of the institutions and attitudes that sustain it.

In the modern age, Arendt believed, politics has been degraded by its subordination to economics, an inversion of the ancient Greek view of the proper relationship between action, work and labour. Politics has become increasingly devoted to promoting the wealth and physical wellbeing of citizens, rather than being the place where great words and immortal deeds are enacted. This is true of both capitalist and socialist systems, which are fundamentally anti-political in the classical sense, as Arendt defines it. Whereas the ancient Greeks relegated all matters of production and consumption to the lower sphere of private life, keeping the public sphere untainted by anything related to labour and work, the moderns are preoccupied with 'political economy', a contradiction in terms to the ancient mind as Arendt understands it, or misunderstands it, as the Athenians in fact often publicly debated the distribution of wealth and taxes. She criticized the French Revolution for concerning itself with issues of social justice, poverty and economic inequality, which lie outside the proper scope of politics, as she saw it. According to her pure, classical understanding of politics, compassion for the suffering of others should be kept out of the public realm, which should be devoted to creating a common world of words and deeds for citizens.

The ideas of Karl Marx are a perfect example of this modern tendency, according to Arendt. She saw his exaltation of labour as yet another symptom of the same anti-political outlook that she had traced back to Plato. Indeed, Marx and Engels believed that, under communism, the state would be unnecessary; it would eventually 'wither away' and be replaced by a self-regulating society of spontaneous co-operation and goodwill. In other words, politics itself would eventually disappear. For Marx, labour is 'the expression of the very humanity of men', whereas for the ancient Greeks it was the least human of activities, according to Arendt. On the capitalist side, John Locke defended the proposition that government has no other end but the preservation of property, consideration of which, for Arendt, should be completely excluded from politics.

When questions of wealth and poverty enter public life, as Arendt argues they increasingly have done in the modern age, genuine politics eventually disappears, as Marx had predicted. In its place we have what she calls society, 'that curious, somewhat hybrid realm between the political and the private'. Society has a herd-like conformity antithetical to the diversity and freedom found in the authentic public sphere. Arendt strongly resisted the intrusion, as she saw it, of social issues into politics and political issues into society – otherwise politics will lose its humanizing character. For example, she considered it no purpose of government to legislate against inequality and discrimination in society. Equality, the 'innermost principle' of the body politic, applies only at the political level, between citizens, and not to the social level, between groups and individuals. Discriminatory practices are legitimate at the level of society, but never at the political level. It was for this reason that Arendt controversially opposed attempts by the state to criminalize racial segregation in the post-war United States, a stance that gained her many enemies on the left. At the same time, she endorsed the American post-war repeal of laws enforcing racial segregation in society, which made her some enemies on the right. Both policies are examples of the inter-penetration of politics and society, which Arendt believed must be resisted if the true character of the political is to be preserved.

No modern thinker has painted a nobler portrait of politics than Arendt, or better understood the grave risks that leaving the care of the public world to others poses. Her idealized image of the ancient Greek city-state, as she saw it, reminds us that, at its best, the political world is a humanizing sphere where great things are possible. It can be a place of courage, inspiring speech, freedom and common action between citizens that elevates us above petty concerns and interests and provides a context for our shared activities and achievements. It is a very salutary lesson for an age that is so deeply and profoundly alienated from politics as ours. But there are so few examples in history where politics of this kind has been practised, or even approximated, that we are bound to wonder if it is intended for a race of heroes rather than ordinary citizens. Even ancient Athens fell short of the ideal, which may be literally utopian. The concrete examples of modern political action that Arendt gives are revolutions, which are exceptional and therefore not a suitable basis for a stable political order. And even modern revolutions have, as often as not, led to political disasters that even Arendt condemned. But having ideals to orient our actions and provide a standard of conduct against which to measure them is surely better than an aimless and empty politics of pure pragmatism.

26

Mao Zedong: The Chairman

The world's largest officially communist state was proclaimed in Tiananmen Square in the heart of Beijing on 1 October 1949 by Mao Zedong, a Marxist peasant and former teacher and librarian from a small village in provincial China. Back in 1921 he had been one of just 13 delegates to attend the first National Congress of the Communist Party of China in a classroom of a girls' school in Shanghai. From that very modest beginning Mao now stood at Beijing's Gate of Heavenly Peace overlooking the packed central square, which thronged with wildly cheering people, as China's new head of state. He had successfully led the country's communists in a civil war that was fought, on and off, for over two decades and now stepped forth as the triumphant ruler of a nation of 500 million people, a quarter of humanity at the time.

From that lofty height Mao would ascend even higher, to cult status, becoming a kind of secular god and the embodiment of the popular will of the Chinese people, at least officially. Millions trekked to Tiananmen Square to attend rallies in honour of 'the Great Helmsman' of the Chinese people, the 'reddest sun in our hearts', as many called him. 'Long live Chairman Mao!' they chanted. 'A long, long life to Chairman Mao!' As a schoolboy in imperial China, he had humbly bowed each morning before a portrait of the revered Confucius with his fellow students. After the revolution his fellow citizens would bow before Mao's portrait every morning. A giant two-storey painting of him still hangs above Tiananmen Square, a short distance from the mausoleum where his embalmed body lies for all to see on the site of what was once the main entrance to the Imperial City.

Ideologically, Mao Zedong was a Marxist–Leninist revolutionary. He read widely and deeply in the works of Karl Marx and his Russian disciple Vladimir Lenin, who had led his own country to socialism in 1917, just before Mao became a committed Marxist. But Mao substantially modified their ideas to suit the particular circumstances of twentieth-century China, thereby creating a distinct political ideology 'produced in Chinese conditions'. Maoism, as it became known, was the official ideology of the Chinese state after 1949. Indeed, Mao's opinions and policies shifted constantly, and he often adapted his ideas to changing circumstances. He prided himself on being a 'dialectical' thinker who openly embraced contradiction as a fundamental feature of both life and thought, making it difficult to specify what exactly is meant by 'Maoism'. Some orthodox Marxists denounce it as a perversion of Marx's ideas, while Mao saw himself as applying the 'universal truths' of Marxism–Leninism to specific Chinese historical conditions.

In the first half of the twentieth century China was not yet a capitalist society; it was still an overwhelmingly poor, rural, semi-feudal peasant society with relatively little industry. As such, it did not meet the material conditions that Marx insisted were necessary for communism, which was only likely after the collapse of mature capitalist industrial economies such as those of France, Germany and Britain (the only ones Marx knew first-hand). For orthodox Marxists China was not yet ripe for communism, which could only rise from the ashes of capitalism after it had first destroyed feudalism and modernized society, unleashing the massive productive forces that would be needed to satisfy everyone's essential needs under communism.

Mao rejected this argument, believing instead that China's relative 'backwardness' was no obstacle to socialism. Indeed, he thought that China would lead the way in building a future global revolutionary order. He argued that, by means of a popular peasant revolution arising in the countryside and guided by the Communist Party, a democratic dictatorship could be established that would use state power to radically transform semi-feudal Chinese society, culture and economics in a 'Great Leap Forward' to communism, something that Marx thought was historically impossible, since politics always follows economics.

Marx also believed that the true bearer of socialist consciousness was the urban, industrial working class, what he called the proletariat. He thought peasants were now historically irrelevant and wrote contemptuously of the 'idiocy of rural life'. Marx lived his whole adult life in large cities in the industrialized West, where capitalism had already substantially destroyed the agrarian peasant class of feudal society. But there was no significant Chinese proletariat in the first half of the twentieth century, which is why it was the last place Marx would have expected a revolution to occur. So Mao looked to the rural peasantry, not the urban workers, as the main revolutionary force in China, since they were 90 per cent of its population. He was himself a peasant's son with a deep mistrust of city life and its sophisticated elite, having never shed the feeling of being a yokel from the provinces, something that he shared with Rousseau, whose *Social Contract* Mao had read as a young man. Both men were deeply suspicious of cities, which Rousseau saw as sources of vice and depravity and Mao considered centres of counter-revolutionary reaction. During China's long civil war Mao led his peasant army from the countryside, and during the 'Cultural Revolution' that he initiated in the mid-1960s he sent urban dwellers out of the cities to learn 'proletarian virtues' from the peasants. His populist strategy was to unleash the vast repressed potential of China's hundreds of millions of long-suffering and desperately poor peasants to overthrow the old regime that was still established in the cities. That is why Maoism has proved so popular with revolutionary socialist groups in the developing world, such as Cambodia's Khmer Rouge and the Shining Path in Peru. For Mao, not all roads to communism will run through capitalism, as Marx and Lenin said they must.

One reason that Mao was not committed to a single path to communism was his belief that history is often shaped by conscious human activity rather than being wholly determined by impersonal economic factors. Unlike Marx, Mao made space for 'subjective factors' such as will power, culture and ideas in the development of political and economic life. This belief provided the ideological underpinning of his two great attempts to transform China: the Great Leap Forward (1958–62) and the Cultural Revolution (1966–76). Mao's preoccupation with 'correct ideological consciousness' reflects his faith in the ability of dedicated revolutionaries to mould social reality in accordance with their ideas, something that orthodox Marxists tend to dismiss.

Negatively, this involved the systematic destruction of traditional Chinese culture and values. 'Destruction before construction' was the slogan. So Mao unleashed a crusade to smash the 'Four Olds': old thought, old culture, old customs and old practices. For example, he modernized traditional customs about marriage, breaking, in his words, 'the feudal shackles that have bound human beings, especially women, for thousands of years'. But that was just the beginning. As with the Protestant Reformation and the Reign of Terror in revolutionary France, a fury of destruction was unleashed during Mao's Cultural Revolution that took even him by surprise. Believing that 'the past oppresses the present', statues and temples were demolished, tombs and monasteries vandalized and books and paintings destroyed on a vast scale by revolutionary zealots. This crusade included an anti-Confucius campaign in which young radicals of the Maoist Red Guards smashed statues of the ancient sage and destroyed the Confucius family cemetery in Qufu, even blowing up the Master's final resting place, the ultimate symbol of traditional feudal China.

Positively, Mao aimed to fill the vacuum left by the 'Four Olds' with the 'Four News': new ideology, new culture, new customs, new habits. He described the Chinese people as 'poor and blank', for on a blank sheet of paper 'the freshest and most beautiful characters can be written, the freshest and most beautiful pictures can be painted'. So streets were renamed in honour of the revolution and its heroes. Mao's zealous wife, Jiang Qing, spearheaded the production of revolutionary new 'model operas' glorifying her husband and the common people in their struggles against foreign and class enemies. These were the only entertainments allowed at the time, shown constantly in schools, factories and fields across China.

Marxism is an inherently internationalist political ideology. Marx held that the working classes of all countries have more in common than the national differences that artificially divide them. He and Lenin hoped for a worldwide revolution leading to global communism. 'Working men have no country', the *Communist Manifesto* tells us. Mao accepted this. But he also believed in integrating internationalism with patriotism, in another of his adaptations of Marxism to Chinese circumstances. He often appealed to Chinese nationalism as a way of mobilizing the peasant masses to oppose global capitalism. And Mao supported national anti-colonial liberation movements around the world for the same reason. Intellectually and ideologically, this combination of nationalism and internationalism presented no problems for a man who openly embraced contradiction and believed that the 'law of the unity of opposites' is 'the fundamental law of the universe'. Stalin also appealed to nationalist sentiments among the Russian people, particularly during the Second World War, while remaining officially committed to the cosmopolitan ideals of communism.

Where Marx, Lenin and Mao were in perfect agreement was in the belief that 'only with guns can the whole world be transformed', as Mao put it. He was as convinced as Lenin that the idealistic ends they shared required brutal means, from which he never flinched. Both were what Machiavelli called 'armed prophets', the highest type of ruler in the estimation of the great Renaissance diplomat, who clearly saw the indispensability of violence to political success. 'A revolution is not a dinner party, or writing an essay, or painting a picture, or doing embroidery', Mao soberly remarked, echoing Machiavelli's view. And he ruled China according to the precept that 'political power grows out of the barrel of a gun'. To get rid of the gun, he advised, it is first necessary to 'take up the gun', which Mao did constantly, both in power and out of it, to build a communist society where no guns would be needed. For Marxists, Leninists and Maoists alike, war, violence and even terror are all legitimate to the degree that they advance humanity towards communism. All readily accepted the very high human cost that would have to be paid to achieve the dream they shared for mankind. Where Confucius had taught harmony, Mao preached 'permanent revolution'. 'Disequilibrium is normal', he believed, whereas 'equilibrium is temporary and relative'. He saw life as pervaded with contradictions that inevitably lead to constant upheaval and conflict, at least until the advent of communism.

Mao believed that class struggle would continue even after the revolution, and might even intensify as residual feudal and bourgeois forces fought back. At the start of the Cultural Revolution he wrote that a violent shake-up of politics and society would be necessary every seven or eight years to revitalize the nation and re-energize its revolutionary spirit, which he feared was being smothered by the institutionalized bureaucratic inertia of post-revolutionary China. For Mao, revolution was not a momentary event but a perpetual struggle between society's contradictory tendencies.

Mao's fear that the revolutionary spirit that he tried so hard to foster in China during the Cultural Revolution – which he viewed as one of his greatest achievements – would fade after his death proved well-founded. As the regime drifted away from communist principles his technocratic successors kept Mao's iconic image but gradually discarded his ideology, resulting in the greatest apparent contradiction of them all for a Marxist: a capitalist economy presided over by a communist state. So, while Mao is still officially honoured in China, Maoism is not. Confucius is officially honoured again, a sure sign that Maoism is losing its grip on the Chinese state. The Great Helmsman warned his colleagues that, if his successors took this erroneous path, then 'our grandsons will certainly rise up in revolt and overthrow their fathers'. There is no sign of that happening now that the generation of Mao's grandson runs China. But China today has one of the highest levels of income inequality in the world, even higher than the United States. If that trend continues, then perhaps Mao's great-grandsons will turn back to the ideas of the man who was the father of modern China.

27

Friedrich Hayek: The Libertarian

In 1974 the Austrian-born British economist Friedrich Hayek was as surprised to receive the Nobel Prize in Economics as the Swedish economist Gunnar Myrdal was to have to share it with him. Hayek was the first champion of free markets to win the prize, which was established in 1969. So controversial was he at the time that the Nobel Committee felt compelled to divide the prize between Hayek and Myrdal, a champion of social democracy and the welfare state. Gunnar Myrdal was a 'Keynesian' advocate of government interventions to stabilize the economy by means of fiscal and monetary policy, even before the pioneering British economist John Maynard Keynes. Hayek, by contrast, was the leading intellectual opponent of Keynesian macroeconomic policies – policies that had been adopted by virtually all post-war democratic nations. In 1974, even US Republican President Richard Nixon was reported to have quipped, 'we are all Keynesians now'.

In the heyday of Keynesian optimism about the ability of the government to manage the economy, Hayek's strong defence of free markets seemed decidedly out of date. Myrdal later ungraciously called for the Nobel Prize in Economics to be abolished rather than given to such a 'reactionary' as Hayek. Yet Hayek had not claimed that the government should never interfere in the economy: he endorsed the public provision of social insurance to protect all citizens from dire poverty. If a pure libertarian restricts government to police and military services, then Hayek was a moderate libertarian. Although Hayek was influenced by some currents of conservative thought, he rejected the label of 'conservative' and considered himself to be a 'classical liberal' in the tradition of Adam Smith. Denounced by social democrats as a reactionary, Hayek was not libertarian enough for many purists. Indeed, the leading libertarian writer of his day, Ayn Rand, denounced Hayek as 'our most pernicious enemy'.

Friedrich August von Hayek was a man of the twentieth century: born in Vienna in 1899, he taught in England and the United States, and died in Freiburg, Germany, in 1992. He always swam against the main currents of his day. In a century consumed by catastrophic nationalism, Hayek remained a cosmopolitan internationalist; in a century of communist, fascist and social-democratic management of the economy, Hayek remained an advocate of free markets; in a century of political centralization, Hayek remained a champion of decentralized political and economic power.

Where did twentieth-century fascists and communists get the idea that they could run the entire economy of a large industrial society? Not from Karl Marx, but from the experience of the First World War: totalitarianism was born from total war. During that conflict, governments both democratic and autocratic imposed draconian controls on political and economic activity in the name of military necessity. The entire economy was conscripted, managed and directed to provide men and material. The realization that a vast, complex modern economy could be run like a single company and turned into an instrument of governmental power changed politics for ever. Dictators found a new source of political power, and social democrats found a new way to promote economic equality. Rather than let markets decide what to produce and at what price, why not let the government make these decisions – for the good of the state, or the party, or the workers?

The experience of another wartime economy – Britain during the Second World War – convinced Hayek that even democratic countries were becoming totalitarian by manipulating the economy and society for political purposes. George Orwell came to the same conclusion from his own experience working for the British government during the war: we should recall that *1984*, Orwell's nightmare vision of the totalitarian future, was inspired less by Hitler or Stalin than by wartime Britain. Hayek's warning about creeping totalitarianism came in the form of his own best-selling book, *The Road To Serfdom* (1944). The temptation to manage the economy for political purposes, argued Hayek, leads us eventually to despotism. Hayek considered plans for the post-war welfare state to be especially insidious because they restricted economic freedom in the name of housing, education and healthcare: the road to selfdom is paved with good intentions.

At the time Hayek wrote his book, he was known by economists mostly for his sharp attacks on the new macroeconomics of Keynes. But despite their differences in economic theory and policy, Keynes shared Hayek's concerns for the future of economic and political liberty in the post-war world. Indeed, Keynes enthusiastically praised

The Road to Serfdom for its robust defence of markets and freedom. Yet, in a letter to Hayek, Keynes pointed out that by rejecting pure libertarianism and permitting a fairly extensive programme of social insurance, Hayek was also on the same slippery slope to serfdom. Hayek, said Keynes, had no principle by which to distinguish between governmental policies that promote freedom and those that destroy it.

In the wake of Keynes's critique, Hayek abandoned economics for the study of political and legal philosophy – through which he hoped to discover a theoretical basis for distinguishing good public law and policy from bad. This enquiry led him into the study of the very foundations of human society, culture and institutions. Hayek rejects the view that human culture is immensely complex because human beings are so intelligent. Rather, he says, the reverse is true: human beings are intelligent (though fallible) mainly because we participate in a complex language and culture. Reason is a social institution, embodied in myriad cultural practices. Hayek agreed with Edmund Burke that individuals are foolish but the species is wise: our own private stock of rationality is puny; we ought to draw upon the bank and capital of our cultural traditions. Our institutions embody much more knowledge and wisdom than we can individually understand or are willing to admit.

Hayek's Burkean argument that markets are wiser than individuals is the basis of his critique of economic planning: no planner (even if armed with super-computers) can ever know as much as all the myriad buyers and sellers. The market incorporates the economic knowledge of millions of producers and consumers: how could a planner have access to all that local, individual knowledge?

Consumers know what they want and what they can afford; producers know their costs and supplies. Much of our economic knowledge is tacit knowledge embodied in our trades, local customs and individual habits. A central planner cannot capture this diverse range of knowledge, which escapes the awareness of individual agents.

Hayek distinguished two kinds of order: the spontaneous order we find in both nature and in culture and then the designed order we find in artefacts or armies. Spontaneous order grows up organically, as does language or morals, while designed order is always deliberately made or imposed. In a spontaneous order, such as the formation of a crystal or a market, we can predict patterns of growth but not where any particular individual element will end up. According to Hayek, this explains why economics will never have the predictive power of physics. Economics is more like biology, which cannot predict the survival of any particular organism but can predict patterns of speciation and extinction. Economists, says Hayek, cannot even predict economic performance, let alone plan for economic targets.

How do these different kinds of order relate to human liberty? A spontaneous order, such as language or the market, has no purpose of its own but merely serves to facilitate the purposes of the individuals who use it. It thus promotes the freedom of individual choice. The designed order of an organization, however, embodies the purposes of its designer: a company or an army imposes the purposes of its leaders upon all its members.

Hayek thus attempts to show that his preference for individual liberty is grounded in the very structure of human knowledge and social order. Free markets create social ecologies of infinite complexity; we should be extremely wary of attempting to manipulate them for transient political purposes, when we don't even understand fully how they function. For example, the global financial crisis of 2008 stemmed in part from the inability of monetary regulators to understand the new kinds of money generated by complex financial instruments. The history of the twentieth century shows how fragile is the ecology of markets, which can easily be destroyed by passing political passions.

Hayek often describes spontaneous and designed social order as if they were mutually exclusive. He tells us that spontaneous order includes 'morals, religion and law, language and writing, money and the market', while designed order includes 'the family, the farm, the plant, the firm, the corporation, and the government'.

Hayek argues that markets grow up spontaneously, while governments are the product of deliberate design. He compares the growth of spontaneous order to the growth of a crystal. Hayek is right that we cannot make a crystal in the sense of putting every molecule into place, but we can create the conditions under which a crystal will form itself. Crystals are deliberately designed as much as they are grown. To grow a crystal in a laboratory, a researcher first designs a matrix in which to structure the growth. That matrix does not determine precisely where each new molecule will be located, but it provides a pattern for their spontaneous growth. In short, a crystal is at once grown and made, spontaneous and designed.

In the same way, constitutions and legislation, by telling us what can be bought and sold (ranging from land to ideas), provide the matrix within which markets can grow – meaning that markets are both spontaneous and designed. Unless we know what can be legally bought and sold, we will ordinarily not risk buying and selling. Modern markets in land, labour and capital were made possible by deliberate legislation abolishing primogeniture, freeing workers from landowners and permitting usury. Markets are created every day by new legislation or regulations: markets in pollution, or in health insurance, or in home schooling. Yes, markets do grow up spontaneously, but only when a legal matrix defining property rights is deliberately made.

According to Hayek, markets promote human liberty because they arise spontaneously to serve our individual purposes; government programmes, by contrast, are deliberately designed to serve the purposes of the governors, constraining individual liberty. Yet Hayek's own example of the growth of crystals shows that social order is always both designed and spontaneous. Modern markets are partly created by legislation, and the modern welfare state itself grew up spontaneously over the past century as a piecemeal response to perceived market failures. Markets and governments are not as sharply opposed as are liberty and coercion.

Hayek is right that the ecology of markets places constraints upon feasible kinds of public policy. But those constraints are consistent with a wide range of policies, ranging from Hayek's own moderate libertarianism to robust social democracy. Hayek rightly warns us against attempting to turn markets into governmental organizations, as tends to happen in wartime. Markets and the economic freedom they make possible will wither in the face of totalitarian centralized planning. At the same time, markets and common law cannot grow up without governments, legislation and courts to enforce property and other rights. But between anarchy and totalitarianism there is a wide range of feasible mixtures of law and legislation, markets and welfare, private initiative and public administration.

Hayek challenges us today to find ways to protect the basic human needs of all citizens without undermining the efficiency of markets. For example, because of rapid technological developments, workers in particular industries often become redundant. What can we do to help them? Governments often attempt to help by offering public subsidies to support the prices of goods produced by those workers or by imposing tariffs on the importation of foreign goods that compete with domestic goods. Hayek insisted that these public policies grossly distort the natural equilibrium of supply and demand, causing great inefficiency. Instead of using price supports or import tariffs to protect domestic industry or agriculture, he argued that we simply guarantee all citizens a basic minimum income. We should protect workers rather than attempt to protect their obsolete jobs. In this way, a dynamic market economy is made compatible with economic security for all.

Hayek claimed that centralized economic planning could never match the sheer productivity of free enterprise – with the possible exception of wartime mobilization. Because Hayek made these arguments during the collapse of capitalism in the Great Depression, he was often ridiculed or ignored. But he lived long enough to see his views vindicated by the collapse of state communism in the Soviet Union, Eastern Europe and China. When it comes to acknowledging the indispensability of markets, we are all Hayekians now.

28

John Rawls: The Liberal

Like Machiavelli, John Rawls was well aware of the central role that luck plays in our lives, for better or for worse. He was personally fortunate to have been born into a professional family who provided him with a stable and comfortable upbringing and a first-class education. But belonging to the affluent middle class of inter-war Baltimore did not insulate his family from tragedy. Both of Rawls's brothers died of illnesses contracted from him when he was unwell; he survived and they did not, something that left him traumatized. In the Second World War he fought in the Pacific, which he also survived when so many around him were killed. He later wrote about passing through the smouldering ruins of Hiroshima soon after it had been destroyed, making him a direct witness to the horrific aftermath of indiscriminate bombing, which he later condemned as a 'very great wrong'. Towards the end of his life Rawls wrote that these wartime experiences, for which he was decorated, had shattered his faith in divine justice. He had been set to begin studying to become an Episcopalian minister before he joined the US Army in 1943, but three years later he was a non-believer. He devoted the rest of his life to the study of moral and political philosophy rather than theology, searching for a secular theory of justice that would neutralize the impact of brute luck on our lives. The product of this search was *A Theory of Justice* (1971), one of the most important and influential works of political philosophy in the twentieth century.

No society will be just, Rawls claims, if it operates like a lottery, where our individual fortunes in life are determined by the random effects of luck. No one has a legitimate claim to the good fortune they may accidentally benefit from, such as natural talents and inherited wealth, just as those with physical handicaps or who suffer misfortune in life do not deserve the bad consequences that may arise from such accidents. These random effects are 'arbitrary from a moral point of view' and therefore should have no bearing on our prospects and opportunities in life, according to Rawls. They are simply not fair. Instead, people should 'agree to share one another's fate' as a way of addressing the arbitrary and uneven impact of luck so that everyone enjoys an equal opportunity to live a good life, however they understand that. Goods and resources should be distributed according to fair principles of justice, not blind chance.

But what might these principles be, and how will we find them? In answering these questions, Rawls invites his readers to consider what distribution of wealth and property they would choose if, under an imaginary 'veil of ignorance', they knew nothing about their own circumstances in life. This thought experiment is intended to get us to consider such principles independently of our personal circumstances, which are likely to skew our judgement towards our own selfish interests. This idea is similar to a courtroom, where jurors are deliberately kept in the dark about irrelevant facts about the defendant so their judgement in the case is not biased. That's why we say that justice is blind: it does not and should not see what is not relevant. If jurors are told some irrelevant but incriminating fact about a defendant during a trial, the judge should instruct them to disregard it. This does not mean that they literally forget it, since it is not possible to will yourself to forget something. But they set knowledge of it aside when deliberating about the case, to ensure fairness. If we do not know where we will end up in society when thinking about justice, then even a selfish person will choose impartially. Rawls calls this 'justice as fairness'.

By this method, a rationally self-interested person would choose the safest option, in case he ends up at the bottom of the heap in an unequal society. That way, he is no worse off than anyone else. Specifically, according to Rawls, reasonable and impartial people under an imaginary 'veil of ignorance' about their position in society would choose two principles of justice to govern the basic structure of the society and ensure a fair distribution of its goods. First, equal liberty for everyone. Second, inequalities would be allowed only where they are of 'the greatest advantage to the least-advantaged members of society' (what he calls the 'difference principle') and there is equal opportunity to hold offices and positions. Equal liberty for Rawls includes basic political rights and freedoms, such as freedom of speech and assembly and voting and running for public office. These are goods we would choose if we knew nothing about ourselves since they are things 'a rational man wants whatever else he wants'. You don't need to know anything about yourself or your position to desire these basic liberties, which Rawls assumes all reasonable people would want. Controversially, he specifically excludes the right to own 'certain kinds of property (e.g. means of production) and freedom of contract as understood by the doctrine of laissez-faire'. So there is no right to own large-scale enterprises and important resources that are the basic components of a modern industrial economy, such as factories, banks and utilities, which together constitute the 'means of production'. Contrary to John Locke, no one has a right to own and dispose of property that they have legitimately (as Locke sees it) acquired in a just society without limit. So inheriting wealth from your rich parents, for example, is unfair, as that is just a matter of good luck, and luck is contrary to justice. Rawls believed that a just society should neutralize the effects of random events on people's life prospects to the degree that this is possible. Justice requires that the basic structure of society be ordered so that accidental advantages and disadvantages are treated as a common asset of the whole society rather than of individuals, which is similar to Marx's idea of communism ('from each according to his abilities, to each according to his needs'). For example, someone born with a physical handicap should not have to bear the extra costs that arise from it, since it is not their fault. Equally, a person born with great natural intelligence should not benefit from this ability, which they have done nothing to deserve. That is why Rawls is seen as a leading example of what is now called 'luck egalitarianism'.

But Rawls is no Marxist. In *A Theory of Justice* he claims that reasonably impartial people under the 'veil of ignorance' would agree to some wealth inequality if (and only if) it improves the wellbeing of the poorest in society. In some circumstances, allowing a few to acquire more than others may grow the economy and thereby improve the circumstances of the least well off if some of it reaches them too. So, for example, letting someone who is particularly talented earn a lot more than others is permissible only if the extra he earns also benefits the poorest in society, perhaps by increasing tax revenues that can be redistributed to the poor in an expanding economy. Unlike Rousseau, Rawls is against rounding down to achieve equality, making everyone poorer in order to make everyone more equal. Rousseau agreed with Socrates that wealth corrupts morals, so he favoured a society that was materially poor (although not desperately so) and equal, something Rawls finds perverse. Rawls's prudence has been viewed by many Marxists and socialists as a sell-out to capitalism. However, he later claimed that liberal principles of justice may actually be incompatible with even a modified form of capitalism.

Since Rawls was mainly concerned about what justice is (basically), he said relatively little about how to implement it. He does tell us that a strong and active state is required, in his words, 'to preserve an approximate justice in distributive shares by means of taxation and the necessary adjustments to the rights of property'. This probably means a progressive income tax and significant restrictions on inheritance, both of which are already normal across the developed world. It also entails laws to regulate prices and prevent concentrations of 'unreasonable market power', also universal (to a greater or lesser degree) in most mature Western economies, although not to the extent that Rawls would like.

It is not surprising that many have concluded that *A Theory of Justice* is an elaborate justification of post-war, welfare-state capitalism as the system most compatible with the principles of justice it defends. However, Rawls later denied this, openly questioning whether the inequalities that such a system produces really are compatible with those principles after all. In his book *Justice as Fairness: A Restatement*, published a year before his death, he argues that no form of capitalism, however modified and regulated, can uphold his two principles of justice; a fair society requires something more radical, what he vaguely calls a 'property-owning democracy' or even a socialist state in which major utilities and enterprises are owned by the government rather than by private individuals. In other words, political liberalism may require a socialist (or social democratic) economy.

A Theory of Justice provoked decades of intense debate among scholars that turned into a veritable industry, dominating academic political philosophy in the English-speaking world for more than a generation. To a considerable extent, liberal political philosophy became indistinguishable from academic political philosophy itself, largely because of Rawls. His ideas proved highly stimulating while narrowing the scope of theorizing about politics. During those years the United States became very much more diverse, posing serious challenges to liberal theory and practice to accommodate an increasingly broad range of belief systems, religions and values. In his next major work, *Political Liberalism*, Rawls addressed these challenges directly.

Contrary to ancient philosophers such as Plato and Aristotle, Rawls thinks it is both unreasonable and unrealistic in diverse societies to expect everyone to agree in principle or in practice on a single form of life that is uniquely good. Reasonable people will disagree on the ends of life. But they can and should still agree on limited *political* principles that will allow them to co-operate peacefully in spite of the deeper metaphysical differences that divide them. Between individuals and communities of belief that accept them, such principles are like the rules of a game agreed between opposing teams and applied impartially by a judge or referee, in the form of the state. The alternatives to this approach are either coercing everyone to submit to one set of comprehensive beliefs or a protracted civil war without limits between competing groups and individuals, like the wars of religion that devastated seventeenth-century Europe. Neither of these options is consistent with an enduringly just and stable society, without which (as Hobbes saw) few other goods in life are possible. The price of lasting social peace in a society divided by diverse values and beliefs is refraining from coercing others into accepting your views, an attitude Rawls dubs 'reasonableness'. This is not relativism, since diversity is still constrained by broad liberal principles of political justice. Nor is it monism, a belief in a single universal form of life for all, since it accepts a diversity of legitimate conceptions of the good life. Rather, it is a middle way between relativism and monism that balances diversity and constraint. Such political liberalism combines a plurality of private beliefs with common public principles, something that Rawls considers the best and fairest way to manage our differences.

But what is reasonable to a liberal like Rawls is not necessarily reasonable to everyone. For example, a person who truly believes in a sacred text whose commandments come from God would probably consider it quite unreasonable to subordinate them to secular principles of justice that prioritize 'a fair scheme of cooperation'. The same is true of someone who believes in an afterlife with the prospect of eternal bliss or everlasting damnation. Anyone who does prioritize liberal political principles that favour peaceful co-existence over the commands of faith is unlikely to need much persuading by Rawls. As for the rest, calling them 'unreasonable' settles little, in theory or in practice, as what counts as reasonable is itself a matter of deep disagreement, and probably always will be. Any attempt to define what is 'reasonable' will end up as a circular argument. Moreover, a political philosophy that requires individuals to separate their private beliefs sharply from public principles is bound to raise questions about its purported neutrality.

John Rawls is often credited with reviving serious political philosophy from the post-war recession it found itself in. He ambitiously addressed the most basic and fundamental questions in politics and ethics with a rare rigour and depth that changed the subject and set the terms of debate about political justice in the English-speaking world in the second half of the twentieth century. He offered the prospect that liberalism might be reconciled conceptually with both political and economic equality and deep cultural and religious diversity, thereby broadening liberalism in novel ways and breathing life into a political ideology that had grown intellectually stale and uninspiring to many. All of this is beyond serious dispute and is the foundation of Rawls's critical importance in the history of political philosophy. But whether justice as fairness and political liberalism prove to be the final word on the mounting challenges that confront liberal societies is far less certain today.

29

Martha Nussbaum: The Self-Developer

As a student at the elite Baldwin School in Bryn Mawr, Pennsylvania, Martha Nussbaum not only learned French, Latin and Greek but also began a lifelong passion for drama. There she wrote, staged and played the lead in a play based upon the life of French Revolutionary Maximilien Robespierre. Already in high school we find many of the qualities that have marked Nussbaum's career as a moral and political philosopher. Her mastery of classical languages has led her to write books about Greek tragedy and about Aristotle; indeed, as we shall see, Aristotle remains her lifelong touchstone. Her passion for drama has led her to develop an insightful dialogue between philosophy and literature: she has always read philosophy in the light of literature and literature in the light of philosophy. Writing a play about Robespierre anticipated her lifelong passion for social justice and political reform – without embracing his infamous use of political terror! From a very early age, she set about developing her own remarkable talents and then devoted her life to advocating for more people to have the opportunities for self-development that she enjoyed at the Baldwin School.

Nussbaum's moral and political thought draws upon the whole Western tradition, from Plato to John Rawls. Like Aristotle, Nussbaum has always argued that the basic goal of moral and political life is the happiness of every individual human being. Again, like Aristotle, she defines happiness not in terms of having happy feelings but in terms of the development of one's potential – what she calls human flourishing. Her whole scholarly life has been dedicated to exploring the meaning of human flourishing. What constitutes a truly happy human life? How do we measure human development? Nussbaum's life as a political activist has been devoted to campaigning for those who have long been unjustly denied opportunities for flourishing, especially women, the poor and the disabled. She has also argued for greater opportunities for the flourishing of non-human animals.

Human happiness or flourishing is more difficult to define than are the obstacles to that condition. Nussbaum's early passion for ancient Greek tragedy introduced her to some of the main obstacles to happiness, such as death, ignorance, betrayal, calumny, war and political persecution. To this ancient list, we moderns could add addiction, divorce, dementia and unjust discrimination. Indeed, there are so many potential obstacles to a happy and flourishing life that we might be tempted to agree with Augustine that we can hope for happiness only in the next life – this life is a time of trial and suffering.

Plato pioneered a strategy for protecting one's flourishing from these dangers: to define happiness purely in terms of moral virtue. Recall that a virtue is an acquired disposition consistently to choose to do the right thing for the right reasons. According to Plato, each human being has a greater or lesser capacity to know what goodness requires and to achieve it. Of course, this capacity will not develop into a stable virtue without our being properly brought up (a matter of luck) and consistently making good choices. Once we acquire these virtues, we identify ourselves with them so that whatever happens to our bodies, or to our families, or to our property, or to our reputation, does not happen to us. Through the discipline of these moral virtues, I am self-sufficient and invulnerable: no evils can reach the inner citadel of my goodwill. We saw that Socrates was happy even while suffering unjust persecution and then execution: no external evil could threaten his unshakeable commitment to doing what is right. Plato's Socrates often says 'better to suffer injustice than to commit injustice': suffering injustice cannot reach the true self, but to commit injustice is to harm oneself – that is, one's virtuous will.

Nussbaum is moved by the power of this Platonic vision of invulnerable moral self-sufficiency, but, ultimately, she rejects it. Following Aristotle, she argues that to be human is to inhabit a body and to love other people, especially friends and family. What this means is that we cannot retreat to an inner spiritual citadel where we are safe. Being human means always being vulnerable to tragedy, because our bodies are fragile and our relationships to those whom we love are also fragile. It is possible to attempt to detach ourselves from property, from reputation, from other people and even from our own bodies – indeed, some degree of such detachment is wise – but ultimately we find happiness and we flourish through these attachments. The Platonic strategy of self-sufficiency may save us from some kinds of tragic suffering but at the price of losing too much of our humanity: a pyrrhic victory, at best.

Aristotle follows Plato by insisting on the necessity of possessing the moral and intellectual virtues for a happy and flourishing life. After all, most human suffering is self-inflicted: our foolish beliefs and our bad choices usually reflect a lack of virtue, which is at least partially our own fault. Nussbaum agrees with Aristotle that developing moral and intellectual virtue is the best way to flourish. But even virtue, while necessary, is not sufficient to guarantee happiness. We remain vulnerable to many evils. It takes courage to embrace a life always held hostage to the danger of tragic suffering, but such courage is necessary for true human flourishing amid family, friends and fellow citizens. What is striking about Nussbaum's approach to these issues is her ability to draw upon the insights found in ancient Greek drama and modern novels, as well as the classic works of philosophy.

Nussbaum's most important contributions to political philosophy have grown out of her collaboration with the economist Amartya Sen. As a student of economic development, Sen has argued that our measures of such development are deeply flawed. Economic progress had long been measured in terms of the growth of income or self-reports of wellbeing, but Sen has insisted that what we should really be attempting to measure are people's capabilities: that is, their ability to actualize valuable human capacities, such as the capacities to read, write and count, the capacities to direct one's own life, make friends and marry, the capacities to play, enjoy nature and appreciate beauty. In other words, economic development should be understood in Aristotelian terms as the objective actualization of valuable human abilities rather than as the acquisition of money or the mere subjective belief that one is happy. A developed society is one in which all citizens actualize essential human capabilities.

Nussbaum was attracted to Sen's Aristotelian approach to economic development. She generalizes his insights into a theory of social justice by arguing that a just society would be one in which every person has access to the resources and opportunities necessary to develop essential human abilities. In most societies, women, the poor, racial minorities and the disabled lack such access; as a consequence, they possess fewer capabilities than more privileged citizens. She points out that one problem with simply asking people whether their lives are going well is that oppressed people often have low expectations. If one does not expect to be literate, or to direct one's own life or to participate in politics, then one does not miss these abilities. But that does not mean, of course, that one would not prefer a life of greater capabilities, if that were possible.

If Nussbaum generalizes Sen's approach to develop a theory of social justice, then she also specifies Sen's approach by actually listing the essential capabilities, which Sen has explicitly refused to do. To be capable is to be able to participate in these goods: life, health, bodily integrity (freedom of movement and from assault), the senses, imagination and thought (education and creativity), emotions (freedom to love and to form attachments), practical reason (freedom of self-direction), relations to other people, relations to other species, play and control over one's environment (rights of political participation and property). A person has a happy and flourishing life to the degree to which she is able to exercise these capabilities, and a just society is one in which everyone has the opportunity to develop them.

Nussbaum's list of capabilities combines the ideas of John Locke and of Karl Marx. Locke and his successors, such as James Madison, emphasize political capabilities, such as rights to freedom of speech, assembly and voting. For them what is essential for a just society is that every citizen be guaranteed basic political liberties – liberties that rest, they assumed, upon the prior right of private property. Marx and his successors, such as Mao, insisted that social justice rests upon basic economic rights such as the right to food, clothing, shelter, healthcare and employment. Without these economic rights, said Marx, liberal political rights are a sham. What good is the right to free speech if I am hungry, sick or unemployed? Notice that Nussbaum's list includes both liberal political rights as well as Marxian economic rights.

Nussbaum's approach to social justice also combines Aristotle and John Rawls. From Aristotle, of course, she takes the view that human flourishing and happiness stem from developing our valuable human capacities into moral and intellectual virtues (what she calls 'capabilities'). From John Rawls, however, Nussbaum adopts the view that a liberal polity should not compel its citizens to become capable or virtuous. Recall that Rawls defended a 'political liberalism' in which a just polity will tolerate a wide variety of ethical and religious ways of life, so long as advocates of those different ways of life do not attempt to coerce anyone. A society guided by the ideals of political liberalism, then, will permit but not require its citizens to pursue Nussbaum's list of capabilities. All that is necessary for social justice is that every citizen should have the resources and opportunity to develop Nussbaum's capabilities, not that they actually do so. According to Aristotle, by contrast, a polity should ensure not only that citizens have the opportunity to exercise these capabilities but that they actually do so. Since human happiness, says Aristotle, rests upon the exercise of human excellence, political leaders have an obligation to ensure that citizens actually do exercise these capabilities, and not waste their lives on trivial amusements.

Aristotle's polity is thus paternalistic and requires its citizens to develop moral and intellectual virtues, even if those citizens do not want to. Nussbaum, following Rawls, rejects this Aristotelian paternalism, except in the case of children. She agrees that children can be compelled to acquire essential capabilities by, for example, compulsory schooling. But, as a Rawlsian liberal, she rejects the right of the government to compel adults to protect their own health, develop their own minds or seek moral virtue. Hence, on Nussbaum's account, a society could be perfectly just in which everyone has the opportunity to develop his or her essential capabilities but no one actually does so.

Martha Nussbaum, in her many books and articles, has taught us a great deal about human flourishing, and its pitfalls. First, she provides a comprehensive account of that flourishing that reflects the bodily, emotional, social and rational aspects of human life. Second, she alerts us to the inescapable vulnerability of human life: all of our abilities are shadowed by disability. Human happiness and dignity are precious because they are so fragile.

In a world in which wealth is the measure of human development, Nussbaum forcefully reminds us that many citizens, even of very affluent societies, cannot exercise basic personal, social or political capabilities – owing to unjust discrimination, poverty, disability or neglect. In a world in which the pursuit of ever higher 'standards of living' may be ecologically unsustainable, she offers a path for development that focuses less on material abundance than on learning, love and citizenship – a path, she says, that is better for human happiness and for our planet.

30

Arne Naess: The Mountaineer

From childhood until his death, Arne Naess spent summers and holidays exploring the mountains east of Bergen, Norway. In the late 1930s, when he was in his twenties, Naess built a simple cabin on a remote mountain perch called Tvergastein – so remote that it took him 62 trips with a horse to carry up the timbers. At 1,500 metres, it was the highest private cabin in Scandinavia and required considerable hiking, snowshoeing or skiing to be reached. Despite a cosmopolitan life of global activism, research, writing and teaching, Naess spent much of his adult life in his mountain hideaway, exploring the local flora and fauna, and reading Plato, Aristotle, Spinoza and Gandhi. He sought to leave a small footprint not only on his beloved mountain but also on the planet Earth – so he ate only vegetables, possessed only necessities and often lived in his cabin without electricity or plumbing and with very little heat. Why would a distinguished philosopher withdraw from the modern world and even largely from human society? Naess had fallen in love with his mountain perch, and this love led him to identify himself with every living creature, from fleas to human beings. He even considered legally changing his own name to Arne Tvergastein.

We never know what we truly have loved until we lose it. Edmund Burke, as you may recall, pioneered conservative political thought in the wake of the French Revolution. There were no 'conservatives' until all moral, religious, social and political traditions came under attack from the revolutionaries of 1789. Similarly, there were no environmentalists, ecologists or conservationists until the Industrial Revolution threatened to destroy the remaining wilderness and even familiar rural landscapes. Just as political conservatives see political change in terms of what is being lost, so many conservationists see economic change in terms of the loss of natural habitats. No one has been more eloquent or influential in mourning what we have lost to modern commerce, industry and technology than Naess, who once chained himself to a waterfall so that it could not be dammed up.

Naess is best known for his concept of 'deep ecology'. According to him, most environmentalists aim to promote merely human values, by reducing pollution to protect human health, conserving resources to protect future consumption and preserving a bit of wilderness for recreation. All of this 'shallow ecology', said Naess, ignores the inherent value of nature quite apart from its effects on human welfare. Deep ecology holds that not only human beings but all living creatures have a right to live and to flourish. Naess was appalled by what he saw as the arrogance of human beings who treat the whole of the natural world as nothing more than a woodpile to be used, destroyed or wasted for our own convenience.

In the Bible, God gives Adam 'dominion' over nature. Naess rejected this ideal of human domination or even stewardship over the natural world. As if humans could possibly know enough to 'manage' the infinite complexity of nature! According to Naess, every significant human attempt to manage nature has backfired, revealing our arrogance and ignorance. Many large dams, for instance, are now being modified or dismantled because of the unforeseen ecological disasters they have created. Industrial agriculture has left deserts and dust storms in its wake. Naess wanted human beings to be good citizens of the Earth, not its masters.

As good citizens of planet Earth, said Naess, we ought to be concerned not just with our own parochial human interests but also with the common good of the whole of nature. What is that common good? Naess followed the seventeenth-century philosopher Benedict Spinoza in arguing that nature is just another word for God. Instead of locating spiritual or divine realities apart from or above nature, Naess believed that divinity is just another aspect of nature. According to Spinoza, the highest human good is the intellectual love of God, which means, said Naess, the loving appreciation of the infinite diversity of life. Every creature, said Spinoza, including human beings, strives to preserve itself and to actualize all of its powers. Naess insisted that the common good of nature is the self-realization of every living organism. Human self-realization uniquely culminates in the capacity to contemplate and to love the totality of nature, of which we are only one small part. What this means, said Naess, is that human beings approach the divine not by turning away from nature but rather by finding our true home within it. Although human beings have always attempted to leave our natural homes by voyages to new continents and now even to new planets, Naess insisted that no one can be truly happy except in intimate relation with a particular natural setting. Thus, Naess rejected modern ideals of globalization, cosmopolitanism and tourism, let alone space travel. He even fought to keep Norway out of the European Union. He implicitly wanted everyone to follow his own example of a lifelong intimate relation to a particular natural place.

Naess's theory of deep ecology and his worship of non-human nature have led other ecologists to call him a mystic, a misanthrope, a fascist and even a Nazi – despite his heroic service resisting the German occupation of Norway. Because human beings pose a unique threat to pristine nature and perhaps even to the future of life on earth, some 'deep ecologists' are indeed strongly misanthropic. They argue that we need more disease, war and poverty to reduce human numbers if the natural world is going to survive. Naess himself agreed that respect for the common good of nature requires a massive reduction in human population to a level of about 100 million. But before Naess became an ecologist he was a disciple of Gandhi's philosophy of non-violence. Gandhi, who tolerated poisonous snakes, spiders and scorpions within his own home, extended the principles of non-violence to the whole of nature. Naess similarly rejected any use of force or coercion to protect nature; he wanted to reduce human numbers only by voluntary family planning. Despite the radical or even violent implications of his own deep ecology, and the malicious rhetoric heaped upon him, Naess was the most peace-loving of activists. He never once resorted to verbal polemics or abuse; instead, he always sought respectful engagement and common ground with his opponents. Everyone who ever met him agreed that he embodied the peace and goodwill that he sought to bring about in the world.

As a young man, Naess was traumatized by the experience of looking through a microscope and observing a flea that had jumped into a bath of acid. Viewing with horror the struggle, suffering and death agony of this flea, Naess became a lifelong vegetarian. His empathetic identification with the suffering flea became a cornerstone of his deep ecology. Instead of asking human beings to sacrifice our interests on behalf of other creatures, Naess asked us to identify with other creatures, to expand our own 'selves' to include the whole of nature. Through this widening of the self, the protection of nature becomes a kind of enlightened self-interest rather than an altruistic self-sacrifice.

Although he occasionally used the language of rights and duties, Naess much preferred to appeal to beauty and joy. He did sometimes refer to the 'right to life' of every creature, implying our 'duty' not to kill them. And he extended Immanuel Kant's famous imperative 'never to treat a person as a mere means but always also as an end' to our treatment of all living organisms. However, in general, Naess was not interested in any kind of ethics, which he viewed as little more than moralistic aggression. He believed that human beings are motivated less by ethical duties than by their understanding of the world. If we came to see ourselves as just one small part of an immense web of life, if we came to see ourselves in nature rather than above it, if we learned to appreciate the complexity and beauty of pristine ecosystems, then we would protect nature out of a feeling of joy rather than a sense of duty. As a Gandhian pacifist, Naess was reluctant to impose moral, let alone legal, duties on other human beings. He preferred to teach by his own example of loving tenderness towards all creatures, great and small. Hence, his rules about killing always include exceptions: 'Never kill another living creature unless you must in order to survive'. He condemns killing for sport but not from hunger. Although he rejects any explicit ranking of organisms, he does implicitly privilege human life.

Naess is often described or denigrated as a 'mystic'. He did not think that language, let alone philosophical argument, could capture our primordial 'awe' in relation to nature. Ultimately, he was a spiritual thinker who claimed that the human wonder before nature must be cultivated before the elaboration of any ecological ethics. Naess himself drew upon Spinoza's pantheism, Buddhism and Gandhian Hinduism in his own spirituality of nature. But he thought that a proper spiritual response to nature could also be found in many other religious traditions.

The word 'nature' evokes very different images in different minds, just as the word 'God' does. Nature can connote a nurturing mother, the cycle of life and relations of interdependence – or nature can connote the struggle for survival, predators and prey, and cycles of extinction. Nature for Naess was ultimately a peaceable kingdom of mutual co-existence and harmony, where, in the biblical vision, 'the lion lies down with the lamb'. Human beings alone, he suggested, are unnatural: our overweening arrogance, our out-of-control fertility and our destructive intelligence pose a unique threat to the harmony of nature. Nature was a garden of paradise until man arrived and overturned the divine order. Unless human beings return to their proper place as but one creature among infinitely many, nature will be destroyed.

Yet, from another, more Darwinian point of view, nature is not a place of peace or harmony at all: every creature is locked into a struggle for survival; every creature produces too many offspring; every creature kills or is killed. Natural history is replete with starvation, death by exposure, relentless predation and extinction. By some accident of random genetic mutation, human beings developed a uniquely powerful combination of intelligence and dexterity, permitting us to become the top predator. In this view, human culture, technology and urbanization are natural adaptations to our ecological niche, permitting us to dominate and subdue all other organisms.

Did human beings ever live in harmony with nature? Naess and other ecologists have claimed that prehistoric and contemporary hunter–gatherers were able to co-exist with nature. But the fossil record suggests otherwise. As soon as these hunter–gatherers migrated to America, for example, they quickly hunted to extinction all the large Ice Age mammals. Human 'destructiveness' (if that is what predation is) has always been limited only by human knowledge and abilities.

According to Karl Marx, human beings by nature transform the natural world into something recognizably human: that is, into a human home. According to Arne Naess, human beings should stop transforming nature and start conforming to it. Are we by nature the masters and possessors of the earth or are we by nature merely fellow citizens among other creatures? These are ultimate religious and philosophical questions which are not likely to be resolved any time soon.

How should we interpret Naess's distinction between deep and shallow ecology? Although he rejected an 'anthropocentric' perspective on nature (what he calls 'shallow ecology'), his own celebration of the joys of communing with nature, of ecological diversity, the flourishing of all species and the harmony of local ecologies – all these reflect distinctively human values. In other words, both deep and shallow ecology understand and appraise nature in relation to human flourishing. Shallow ecology values nature only insofar as nature serves material or transient human desires. Deep ecology values nature insofar as nature serves the spiritual and permanent human desires for the contemplation of the beautiful and the sublime, for the wonder of the intellectual complexity of natural order and for humility in the presence of a mysterious gift not created by us.

Conclusion: The Unhappy Marriage of Politics and Philosophy

When considering the long history of political thought, it is natural to wonder whether ideas make any difference in the real world. Karl Marx, for one, thought not, and his view has some plausibility. There was political activity long before there was philosophizing about it. Human beings typically act before they think about acting; indeed, we theorize mainly because of the need to overcome obstacles to our practical goals. I only think about how locks work when I cannot get my key to open one. Perhaps philosophy helps us to see more clearly the target that we were already attempting to hit, to use Aristotle's image of archery. By thinking through such vague concepts as liberty, equality and justice, philosophers can help us to pursue those ideals with better focus. Unfortunately, as we have seen, philosophers hold incompatible views of these ideals. How can we improve our aim when our archery masters want us to aim at different targets? We might do better without any teachers at all.

Worse, says Nietzsche, the very act of thinking might undermine effective politics. Bold leadership and decisive action, after all, require certainty and confidence, and philosophy leads us towards doubt, reflection and hesitancy. Shakespeare's Hamlet, after all, studied philosophy, which may explain his famous inability to act; he thinks so much about what he ought to do that he finds it very difficult to do anything. If philosophy made for better politics, then one would expect philosophers to be good rulers. But, apart from Plato, most people think that philosophers would make sorry and indecisive rulers, or worse (sometimes much worse).

We might instead think of our political philosophers as visionaries or prophets of the political future, concerned less with where we are now than with where we should be going. In this sense, they are like other great innovators: Leonardo da Vinci, for example, imagined aeroplanes and submarines long before they were feasible in practice. Perhaps our great political thinkers are visionaries who imagine new kinds of politics which are put into practice only much later, if at all. Confucius, for example, proposed that kings ought to listen to literary scholars before making public policy. Lo and behold, a few centuries later China instituted a system of civil service examinations designed to fill the imperial bureaucracy with literary scholars. Plato envisaged a communism that inspired Marx, Lenin and Mao; his proposal to eliminate the nuclear family inspired Israeli kibbutzim and continues to inspire some radical feminists to this day. Al-Farabi imagined imams who were also philosophers, just as Maimonides imagined philosophers who were also rabbis.

Some political ideas have indeed been prophetic. At a time when Italy was divided into dozens of separate kingdoms and republics, Machiavelli called for a united Italy in 1513. It would take Italy 350 years finally to achieve unification. At a time when Europe was dominated by hundreds of hereditary monarchies constantly at war with each other, Kant foresaw a continent of constitutional republics that never go to war, 150 years before the establishment of the European Union. Rousseau predicted a coming 'age of revolutions' in Europe 25 years before the violent overthrow of the Old Regime in France that changed the course of European history. Burke predicted a reign of terror and a military dictatorship years before Robespierre or Napoleon had arrived. At a time when the world was dominated by Britain and France, Tocqueville predicted that one day the entire globe would be divided between the United States and Russia, as it was during the Cold War.

Some political ideas have been rather less prophetic. Marx famously predicted the 'unavoidable' collapse of capitalism. Few today would describe the United States Constitution that Madison helped to write in the eighteenth century as the ideal framework for a massive, complex industrial and post-industrial society. Kant's age of 'perpetual peace' is nowhere in evidence. Paine's insistence that monarchies always tend towards tyranny is contradicted by the peaceful, democratic constitutional monarchies of Canada, Australia, New Zealand and northern Europe, all of which are more equal societies than the United States that he saw as the beacon of progress for humanity.

Some of the visions of our political philosophers are so dark that we can only hope they are not prophetic. Rousseau, Tocqueville, Nietzsche and Arendt all worried about a future in which the citizens of advanced industrial democracies would become so safe and comfortable that they would happily surrender their hard-won political freedom for the fleeting pleasures of mass entertainment and shopping. Perhaps politics itself will become obsolete in a globalized world of private consumption administered by interlocking elites and governed by no one. Or, in Naess's nightmare, having destroyed the planet by the greedy and violent exploitation of nature, human beings will be forced to live in exile by colonizing outer space.

Although there is some evidence for the view that it has a prophetic role in imagining new kinds of politics (both positive and negative), political philosophy is about the past as much as it is about the future. Even those aspects of it which seem most innovative often take their inspiration from history. In proposing that scholars should advise kings, Confucius claimed to be looking back to the era of the great 'sage-kings'. Plato's radical vision of communism seems to be inspired by the ancient Egyptian caste hierarchy of priests, warriors and workers. Augustine, Al-Farabi and Maimonides all looked back to ancient Scripture for models of government, and Aquinas looked back both to Moses and to Aristotle. Arendt insisted that modern citizens should act in the public forum with the courage of ancient Athenians, and Machiavelli's dream of a unified Italy was one that also restored the grandeur of ancient Rome.

Some of our political philosophers attempted to escape all influence from the past, though usually we can clearly see the historical sources of their ideals. Hobbes, Locke, Rousseau, Kant and Rawls all devised thought experiments in which pre-political human beings would come to agreement about a purely rational set of rights. They were interested not in what rights people actually had but in what rights people ought to have in a purely rational and just society. Yet, notoriously, the rights that 'reason' supposedly demands turn out to track closely the history of English common-law liberties against the Crown acquired piecemeal over time, going back to Magna Carta in 1215. The abstract schemes of purely 'rational' rights devised by our political philosophers often refine and make more universal the rights that Englishmen have inherited from the past. In this respect, the American Revolution looks less like a break with the past than an insistence that England respect traditional English liberties in her American colonies. Those philosophers who presume to use reason to escape history usually end up repeating history.

Politics and philosophy will always sit uneasily together, since they seek different, and sometimes incompatible, things. That is why so many philosophers have been persecuted for their political beliefs. This problem was present at the very beginning of Western civilization when the citizens of ancient Athens sentenced their greatest philosopher, Socrates, to death for corrupting the youth of the city with his radical ideas. Machiavelli, Paine, Gandhi and Qutb were imprisoned; and Confucius, Aristotle, Maimonides, Hobbes, Locke, Rousseau, Marx and Arendt were exiled. It is only relatively recently in the history of the West that it has been safe to speak and write openly about politics. Such freedom is a hard-won modern achievement, remains precarious and still has many enemies.

The ideas of these thinkers are sometimes dangerous to politics too. The ancient Athenians condemned Socrates for a reason: they believed that he was recklessly undermining their city and subordinating its interests to his personal quest for truth. Ideas can lead to perverse consequences that may be practically destructive. It is often very hard, perhaps impossible, to predict how they will develop when they enter the real world and take on a life of their own. For example, Rousseau's theories about political virtue inspired radical Jacobins, who used them to justify a reign of terror against the enemies of the French Revolution, as they saw them. Both Lenin in Russia and Mao in China claimed to be acting according to the ideas of Marx when they relied on widespread violence and coercion to maintain the regimes they established. And we have seen how the Nazis attempted to appropriate the ideas of Nietzsche to support their inhuman policies. Plato, Marx and Rousseau have all, at times, been blamed for totalitarianism.

The difficult relationship between philosophy and politics recalls the parable of the porcupines, which come together in the cold for mutual warmth but pull away from each other when pricked by their sharp spines. They need each other but cannot bear each other. They provide mutual comfort but only by causing mutual pain. Like porcupines, politics and philosophy are mutually beneficial and mutually threatening. In the end, the porcupines decide that it is best to remain fairly close but at a little distance from one another. A little less warmth means a little less pain. No pain means the possibility of freezing to death.

Politics and philosophy are stuck with each other and, on balance, that's a good thing, in spite of the risks that each poses to the other. There is no political system that is wholly devoid of ideas, and philosophical reflection on politics is as unavoidable as thinking itself. For its part, philosophy does not exist in an otherworldly realm remote from the real world. It flourishes only within political systems that provide a minimum of peace and stability conducive to reflection. As Hobbes wrote, 'Leisure is the mother of Philosophy, and Common-wealth the mother of Peace and Leisure: Where first were great and flourishing Cities, there was first the study of Philosophy'. If Hobbes is right that politics is the pre-condition for philosophy, then philosophy must study politics to better preserve itself. Perhaps that is why Socrates refused to escape from prison where he was being held before his execution; when his wealthy friend Crito offered to arrange it, Socrates declined out of respect for the law, even though he was about to be put to death in its name. And at the trial that led to his death, Socrates defended philosophy as necessary for the good of the state. Philosophy questions the things that are taken for granted in politics, not merely to understand them better but also to make them better, often by imagining new political ideals, systems, principles of justice and forms of life. Without it, politics really would be just a swamp.

SUGGESTED FURTHER READING

We have listed the most important political works of each thinker below. For the ancients and medievals, we have recommended excellent modern English-language translations. For the moderns and contemporaries, we have put the first date of publication for each work in brackets rather than details of specific English translations, since there are many of these that are widely available. We have also listed a biography for each thinker, where they exist.

ANCIENTS

Confucius
The Analects, translated by D. C. Lau (Penguin Classics, 1979)
Mencius, translated by D. C. Lau (Penguin Classics, 2005)

Plato
The Trial and Death of Socrates, translated by G. M. A. Grube (Hackett, 2000)
Republic, translated by C. D. C. Reeve (Hackett, 2004)
Statesman, translated by Eva Brann et al. (Focus Philosophical Library, 2012)
The Laws, translated by Trevor Saunders (Penguin Classics, 2004)

Aristotle
Nicomachean Ethics, translated by Terrence Irwin (Hackett, 1999)
Politics, translated by C. D. C. Reeve (Hackett, 2017)

Augustine

Political Writings, translated by Michael Tkacz and Douglas Kries (Hackett, 1994)

City of God, edited and abridged by Vernon Bourke (Image Books, 1958)

MEDIEVALS

Al-Farabi

Medieval Political Philosophy: A Sourcebook, edited by Joshua Parens and Joseph Macfarland (Cornell University Press, 2011)

The Philosophy of Plato and Aristotle, translated by Muhsin Mahdi (Cornell University Press, 2001)

Maimonides

Medieval Political Philosophy: A Sourcebook, edited by Joshua Parens and Joseph Macfarland (Cornell University Press, 2011)

The Guide of the Perplexed, edited and abridged by Julius Guttmann (Hackett, 1995)

Thomas Aquinas

On Law, Morality, and Politics, translated by Richard Regan (Hackett, 2002)

St. Thomas Aquinas on Politics and Ethics, translated by Paul Sigmund (Norton, 1988)

MODERNS

Niccolò Machiavelli

The Discourses on Livy (1531)

The Prince (1532)

Maurizio Viroli, *Niccolò's Smile: A Biography of Machiavelli* (2000)

Thomas Hobbes

De Cive ('On the Citizen') (1642)

The Elements of Law (1650)

Leviathan (1651)
Behemoth (1679)
A. P. Martinich, *Hobbes: A Biography* (1999)

John Locke
Second Treatise of Government (1689)
A Letter Concerning Toleration (1689)
Maurice Cranston, *John Locke: A Biography* (1957)

David Hume
A Treatise of Human Nature (1738–40)
Essays, Moral and Political (1741)
An Enquiry Concerning the Principles of Morals (1751)
The History of England (1754–61)
Dialogues Concerning Natural Religion (1779)
Roderick Graham, *The Great Infidel: A Life of David Hume* (2004)

Jean-Jacques Rousseau
A Discourse on the Origins of Inequality (1755)
The Social Contract (1762)
Leo Damrosch, *Jean-Jacques Rousseau: Restless Genius* (2005)

Edmund Burke
Reflections on the Revolution in France (1790)
An Appeal From the New to the Old Whigs (1791)
Letters on a Regicide Peace (1795–7)
Conor Cruise O'Brien, *The Great Melody: A Thematic Biography of Edmund Burke* (1992)

Mary Wollstonecraft
A Vindication of the Rights of Men (1790)
A Vindication of the Rights of Woman (1792)
Janet Todd, *Mary Wollstonecraft: A Revolutionary Life* (2000)

Immanuel Kant
An Answer to the Question: "What is Enlightenment"? (1784)
Groundwork of the Metaphysics of Morals (1785)
Perpetual Peace: A Philosophical Sketch (1795)
The Metaphysics of Morals (1797)
Manfred Kuehn, *Kant: A Biography* (2001)

Thomas Paine
Common Sense (1776)
The Rights of Man (1791–2)
The Age of Reason (1794–1796)
Agrarian Justice (1797)
John Keane, *Tom Paine: A Political Life* (1995)

G. W. F. Hegel
Philosophy of Mind (1817)
Elements of the Philosophy of Right (1820)
Terry Pinkard, *Hegel: A Biography* (2001)

James Madison
The Federalist Papers, especially numbers 10 and 51 (1788)
Memorial and Remonstrance against Religious Assessments (1785)
Noah Feldman, *The Three Lives of James Madison: Genius, Partisan, and President* (2017)

Alexis de Tocqueville
Democracy in America (1840)
The Old Regime and the French Revolution (1856)
André Jardin, *Alexis de Tocqueville: A Biography* (1984)

John Stuart Mill
On Liberty (1859)
Considerations on Representative Government (1861)
Utilitarianism (1863)

The Subjection of Women (1869)
Richard Reeves, *John Stuart Mill: Victorian Firebrand* (2007)

Karl Marx
The Manifesto of the Communist Party (1848)
The Eighteenth Brumaire of Louis Napoleon (1852)
The Civil War in France (1871)
Critique of the Gotha Programme (1875)
Capital, 3 volumes (1867–94)
The German Ideology (1932)
Francis Wheen, *Karl Marx* (1999)

Friedrich Nietzsche
Thus Spoke Zarathustra (1883)
On the Genealogy of Morality (1887)
The Will to Power (1901)
Julian Young, *Friedrich Nietzsche: A Philosophical Biography* (2010)

CONTEMPORARIES

Mohandas Gandhi
Non-Violent Resistance (Satyagraha) (1951)
Autobiography (1927)
Ved Mehta, *Mahatma Gandhi and His Apostles* (1976)

Sayyid Qutb
The Sayyid Qutb Reader, edited by Albert Bergesen (2008)
Social Justice in Islam (1949)
Milestones (1964)
James Toth, *Sayyid Qutb: The Life and Legacy of a Radical Islamic Intellectual* (2013)

Hannah Arendt
The Origins of Totalitarianism (1951)
The Human Condition (1958)
Eichmann in Jerusalem (1963)
Anne Conover Heller, *Hannah Arendt: A Life in Dark Times* (2015)

Mao Zedong
On Contradiction (1937)
Quotations from Chairman Mao Tse-Tung (the 'Little Red
    Book') (1964)
Philip Short, *Mao: A Life* (1999)

Friedrich Hayek
The Road to Serfdom (1944)
Law, Legislation, and Liberty (1973)
The Fatal Conceit (1988)
Alan Ebenstein, *Friedrich Hayek: A Biography* (2001)

John Rawls
A Theory of Justice (1971)
Political Liberalism (1993)
Justice as Fairness: A Restatement (2001)
Thomas Pogge, *John Rawls* (2007), chapter 1

Martha Nussbaum
The Fragility of Goodness (1986)
Creating Capabilities: The Human Development Approach (2011)

Arne Naess
Ecology of Wisdom: Writings of Arne Naess (2008)
Life's Philosophy: Reason and Feeling in a Deeper World (2002)

ACKNOWLEDGEMENTS

In writing this book we have incurred many debts that we are pleased to acknowledge here.

Graeme Garrard
I am grateful to Cardiff University for granting me study leave to work on this book, and to Clare Hall, Cambridge, where it was first conceived and begun while I was a Visiting Fellow.

Drafts of several of the chapters I wrote were read and much improved by constructive comments from Ronald Beiner, Tobias Pantlin, David Rezvani, Peter Sedgwick, Cherrie Summers and Howard Williams. I very much appreciate the time and care they all gave to this.

I have been fortunate to have some very supportive friends and colleagues who have enriched my working life, foremost among whom are Matteo Bonotti, David Boucher, Andrew Dowling, David Hanley, Sean Loughlin, Nick Parsons, Lewis Paul Buley, Carole Pateman and Craig Patterson.

My first serious study of political ideas began as an undergraduate at the University of Toronto with Ronald Beiner. He inspired my interest in the subject then, and he has been my model of what a scholar should be ever since.

Finally, and above all, I could not have asked for a better co-author, critic and friend than James Bernard Murphy.

James Bernard Murphy

I discovered political philosophy in 1976 in the Directed Studies Program at Yale University, where I also received my doctorate in 1990.

I am equally indebted to Dartmouth College, where I have had the privilege to teach political ideas to many brilliant students, who have challenged me, kept me honest about the limits of my knowledge and inspired me with their youthful passion. In particular, I wish to thank my students who proofread the manuscript of this book: Natalia McLaren, Katarina Nesic, Josie Pearce and Joseph Torsella.

No one has taught me more about political philosophy or about friendship than my co-author, Graeme Garrard.

I owe a deep debt of gratitude to my wife, Kirsten Giebutowski, who generously read my chapters. Whatever literary merits they may possess are due to her careful editing.

We have divided the thinkers profiled here equally between us, with James Murphy writing about all of the ancient and medieval authors (from Confucius to Aquinas) and some of the moderns and contemporaries (Hegel, Madison, Tocqueville, Gandhi, Qutb, Hayek, Nussbaum and Naess). Graeme Garrard wrote about the rest.

We are both very grateful to our agent, Jaime Marshall, and our Bloomsbury editor, Jamie Birkett, for their tremendous advice, encouragement and sagacity.

INDEX

INDEX

Al-Ghazali 48
Godwin, Mary 128
Goethe, Johann Wolfgang von 197
goods
    goods of human life 87–9, 90
    hierarchy of goods 31–2
government 5–7, 34, 40, 51, 54,
        83–4, 106, 176, 177, 189, 218,
        229, 261
    Aristotle 91
    Augustine 41, 42–3
    Burke 121, 122, 123–4
    Confucius 13, 18, 19
    and economy 239–41
    Hayek 240, 244, 245–6
    Hobbes 91
    Kant 136, 138, 139, 140–1
    Locke 94–8, 99
    Madison 160, 161–3, 164, 165–6
    Paine 146–7, 148, 149
    Plato 26–7
    Tocqueville 172–3
    USA 64, 113–14, 146–7, 159,
        160, 161–4, 165–6, 169

happiness (human flourishing) 256
    Aristotle 32, 87, 258, 260–1
    Kant 139–40
    Nussbaum 256–7, 258, 259–61
    Plato 256–7
    Qutb 216–17
Hayek, Friedrich August von
        239–46
Hegel, Georg Wilhelm Friedrich
        151–7
heresy, persecution of 42
*Historical and Moral View of
    the Origin and Progress of
    the French Revolution, An*
    (Wollstonecraft) 128

History of England (Hume) 103,
    107
Hitler, Adolf 153, 154, 199–200
Hitler as Nobody Knows Him
    (Hoffmann) 200
Hobbes, Thomas 41, 85–92, 97,
        111, 113, 114, 147, 227,
        274–5, 277
Hoffmann, Heinrich 200
Human Condition, The (Arendt)
    225
human flourishing, *see* happiness
human life 226–7
human rights 99
humanism 49, 54, 55, 69, 72
Hume, David 101–8, 112, 148–50,
    162

imaginative perfection 62
income inequality 238
Index of Forbidden Books, Vatican
    111
India 177, 192, 205–206
individualism 177–83
inequality 50–1, 173, 192, 228, 238,
    250
injustice 257: *see also* justice
intellectual perfection 62
International Workingmen's
    Association 189
internationalism 236
is/ought fallacy 104–5
Islam
    medieval Islam 47–55
    militant Islam 215–21
Italy 273

Jefferson, Thomas 34, 43, 98, 107,
    113–14, 120, 159, 160, 162,
    180

monarchy 34, 93, 145, 273, 275
monism 253
moral absolutism 135–42
moral equality 170
moral idealism 141
moral nihilism 201
moral sentiments 104–5
morality 137–8, 194, 196
Moses 51, 62–3, 64
Myrdal, Gunnar 239–40
mysticism 151–7

Naess, Arne 9, 263–70, 274
Napoleon 151, 152–3, 197–8
Napoleonic code 63
Nasser, Gamal 215
national unity 53
nationalism 59, 227, 236
natural justice 121
naturalism 105
naturalistic fallacy 104–5
nature, human beings and 268–9
Nazism 199–200, 211
Neoplatonism 49
Nicomachean Ethics (Aristotle) 31
Nielsen, Kai 81
Nietzsche, Friedrich 52, 193–201, 272
nihilism 201
Nixon, Richard 239
non-violence 205–8, 209–12, 266: *see also* violence
Nussbaum, Martha 139, 255–62

oligarchy 33
On Free Will (Augustine) 40
On Liberty (Mill) 179, 181–2
On the Subjection of Women (Mill) 178–9

order 243–5
Origins of Totalitarianism, The (Arendt) 223
Orwell, George 241

pacifism 211
paganism 37, 38, 40, 219
Paine, Thomas 8, 121, 130, 143–50, 273, 275
  and French Revolution 128, 143–4
participatory democracy 140
paternalism 126, 139, 181, 227, 261
Paul, St 40
perfection 62
philosophical radicalism 106
physics 30
pity 105
Plato 8, 21–7, 30–1, 38–9, 49, 53, 122, 133, 272
  beautiful goodness 15
  communism and 272, 274
  and democracy 173
  happiness 256–7
  wisdom 50
poleis (city-states) 32–3
political economy 227–8
political liberalism 260
Political Liberalism (Rawls) 252
political radicalism 106
Politics (Aristotle) 32, 33, 49–50, 53, 54, 80
polities 33, 34, 40, 52–3, 260–1
power 4–7
practical reason 31
practical wisdom 50
Price, Richard 123
Prince, The (*Il principe*, Machiavelli) 77–8, 79, 80, 81, 82, 83, 84

A NOTE ON THE AUTHORS

Graeme Garrard has taught political thought at Cardiff University, UK since 1995 and at the Harvard Summer School, USA since 2006. He has lectured at colleges and universities in Canada, the United States, Britain and France for 25 years. He is the author of two books: *Rousseau's Counter-Enlightenment* (2000) and *Counter-Enlightenments: From the Eighteenth Century to the Present* (2006).

James Bernard Murphy is Professor of Government at Dartmouth College, Hanover, New Hampshire, USA where he has taught since 1990. His newest book is tentatively titled *Your Whole Life: Childhood and Adulthood in Dialogue* (University of Pennsylvania Press, 2020).

A NOTE ON THE TYPE

The text of this book is set in Minion, a digital typeface designed by Robert Slimbach in 1990 for Adobe Systems. The name comes from the traditional naming system for type sizes, in which minion is between nonpareil and brevier. It is inspired by late Renaissance-era type.